DISCOVERING CAREERS

Health

**Titles in the
Discovering Careers
series**

**Adventure
Animals
Computers
Construction
Environment
Health
Math
Nature
Science
Space Exploration
Sports
Transportation**

DISCOVERING CAREERS

Health

Ferguson's
An Infobase Learning Company

Discovering Careers: Health

[handwritten: 610.69 Facts]

Copyright © 2011 by Infobase Learning

Ferguson's
An imprint of Infobase Learning
132 West 31st Street
New York NY 10001

Library of Congress Cataloging-in-Publication Data

Health.
    p. cm. — (Discovering careers)
  Includes bibliographical references and index.
  ISBN-13: 978-0-8160-8051-9 (hardcover : alk. paper)
  ISBN-10: 0-8160-8051-8 (hardcover : alk. paper) 1. Medicine—Vocational guidance—Juvenile literature. 2. Allied health personnel—Vocational guidance—Juvenile literature.
  R690.H395 2011
  610.69023—dc22
                  2010040587

Ferguson's books are available at special discounts when purchased in bulk quantities for businesses, associations, institutions, or sales promotions. Please call our Special Sales Department in New York at (212) 967-8800 or (800) 322-8755.

You can find Ferguson's on the World Wide Web at http://ferguson.infobase publishing.com

Text design by Erika K. Arroyo and Erik Lindstrom
Composition by Erik Lindstrom
Cover printed by Bang Printing, Brainerd, Minn.
Book printed and bound by Bang Printing, Brainerd, Minn.
Date printed: March 2011
Printed in the United States of America

10 9 8 7 6 5 4 3 2 1

CONTENTS

Introduction

You may not have decided yet what you want to be in the future. And you don't have to decide right away. You do know that right now you are interested in medicine and health care. Do any of the statements below describe you? If so, you may want to begin thinking about what a career in health care might mean for you.

___ Science is my favorite subject in school.
___ I like to do science experiments.
___ I like health class.
___ I am interested in nutrition.
___ I like to take care of people.
___ I like to help people with disabilities.
___ I am interested in the human body and how it works.
___ I collect specimens to view under my microscope.
___ I like to help people solve problems.
___ I am curious about how things work.
___ I am good at observing small details.
___ I like to fix and build things.
___ I would like to find a cure for cancer or AIDS.
___ I like to babysit my younger brothers and sisters.
___ I am interested in learning first aid and CPR.
___ Physical fitness and proper diet are important to me.

Discovering Careers: Health is a book about careers in health care and medicine, from advanced practice nurses to psychiatrists. The health care field is growing rapidly. In fact, it is one of the fastest-growing industries in the United States. Health care workers are employed in hospitals, clinics, medical offices, hospices, nursing homes, and home care settings. They also work in schools, universities, research labs, pharmaceutical companies, cosmetic companies, food processing plants, and in all types of industry making sure other workers stay safe and healthy.

This book describes many possibilities for future careers in medicine and health care. Read through it and see how different careers are connected. For example, if you are interested in nursing, you will want to read the chapters on Advanced Practice Nurses, Nurses, Nurse Assistants, and Home Health Care Aides. If you are interested in technical careers, you will want to read the chapters on Biomedical Engineers and Biomedical Equipment Technicians. If you want to help organize and manage medical records, you should read the chapters on Medical Record Technicians and Medical Secretaries. If you want to become a doctor, you should read the chapters on Chiropractors, Dentists, Physicians, and Psychiatrists. Go ahead and explore!

What Do Health Workers Do?

The first section of each chapter begins with a heading such as "What Physical Therapists Do" or "What Orthotists and Prosthetists Do." It tells what it's like to work at this job. It describes typical responsibilities and assignments. You will find out about working conditions. Which health care professionals work in hospitals and laboratories? Which ones travel for their jobs? This section answers all these questions.

How Do I Become a Health Worker?

The "Education and Training" section tells you what schooling you need for employment in each job—a high school diploma, training at a junior college, a college degree, or a medical degree. It also talks about on-the-job training that you could expect to receive after you're hired, and whether or not you must complete an apprenticeship program.

How Much Do Health Workers Earn?

This section gives the average salary figures for the job described in the chapter. These figures provide you with a general idea of how much money people with this job can make. Keep in mind that many people really earn more or less than the amounts given here because actual salaries depend on many different things, such as the size of the company, the location of the company, and the amount of education, training, and experience you have. Generally, but not always, bigger hospitals and medical facilities located in major cities pay more than smaller ones in smaller cities and towns, and people with more education, training, and experience earn more. Also remember that these figures are current averages. They will probably be different by the time you are ready to enter the workforce.

What Will the Future Be Like for Health Workers?

The "Outlook" section discusses the employment outlook for each career: whether the total number of people employed in this career will increase or decrease in the coming years and whether jobs in this field will be easy or hard to find. These predictions are based on economic conditions, the size and makeup of the population, and new technology.

Keep in mind that these predictions are general statements. No one knows for sure what the future will be like. Also remember that the employment outlook is a general statement about an industry and does not necessarily apply to everyone. A determined and talented person may be able to find a job in an industry or career with the worst kind of outlook. And a person without ambition and the proper training will find it difficult to find a job in even a booming industry or career field.

Where Can I Find More Information?

Each chapter includes a sidebar called "For More Info." It lists organizations that you can contact to find out more about the field and careers in the field. You will find names, addresses, phone numbers, e-mail addresses, and Web sites.

Extras

Every chapter has a few extras. There are photos that show health workers in action. There are sidebars and notes on ways to explore the field, interesting facts, profiles of people in the field, tips on important skills for success in the field, information on work settings, lists of Web sites and books, and other resources that might be helpful.

At the end of the book you will find three additional sections: "Glossary," "Browse and Learn More," and "Index." The Glossary gives brief definitions of words that relate to education, career training, or employment that you may be unfamiliar with. The Browse and Learn More section lists health-related books, periodicals, and Web sites to explore. The Index includes all the job titles mentioned in the book.

It's not too soon to think about your future. We hope you discover several possible career choices. Happy hunting!

Advanced Practice Nurses

What Advanced Practice Nurses Do

You have seen registered nurses at school, in hospitals, at the doctor's office, and in other settings. But did you know that there are other types of registered nurses (R.N.s) called *advanced practice nurses*? These nurses have received extra college training and have a lot of responsibility. There are four types of advanced practice nurses: *nurse practitioners, certified nurse-midwives, nurse anesthetists,* and *clinical nurse specialists.*

EXPLORING

- Take a first aid class.
- Offer to help care for a sick grandparent or elderly neighbor.
- Read books about nursing. Although most books about advanced practice nursing are geared toward college students, you can read books about general nursing. Here are a few suggestions: *A Career in Nursing: Is It Right For Me?,* by Janet Katz (Mosby, 2007) and *Your Career in Nursing: Manage Your Future in the Changing World of Healthcare,* 5th edition, by Annette Vallano (Kaplan Publishing, 2008).
- Ask your health teacher to arrange an information interview with an advanced practice nurse.

A nurse practitioner writes a prescription for a patient. (John Raoux, AP Photo)

Nurse practitioners have many duties. They conduct physicals, diagnose and treat common illnesses, and order tests and X-rays. In many states they can even prescribe drugs. Nurse practitioners regularly report a patient's treatment plan to a physician. They sometimes send patients to physicians for further care or treatment. Some states allow nurse practitioners to function without supervision by a physician. Nurse practitioners specialize in many areas. *Family nurse practitioners* provide primary care to people of all ages. *Pediatric nurse practitioners* provide primary health care for infants through adolescents. *Gerontological nurse practitioners* are often based in nursing homes and work with older adults. *School nurse practitioners* work in school settings and provide primary health care for students. *Occupational health nurse practitioners* focus on employment-related health problems and injuries. *Psychiatric nurse practitioners* work with people who have mental or emotional problems. *Women's health care nurse practitioners* provide primary care for women from adolescence through old age.

Certified nurse-midwives provide care to expectant mothers and to women with gynecological problems. They work under the supervision of obstetricians. Certified nurse-midwives teach pregnant women

DID YOU KNOW?

Nursing isn't just for women. Approximately 6 percent of nurses are males, and the number of men who become nurses is slowly increasing. Most male nurses work in critical care, emergency care, surgery, medical management, education, and as nurse practitioners. For more information about careers for men in nursing, contact The American Assembly for Men in Nursing (PO Box 130220, Birmingham, AL 35213-0220, aamn@aamn.org, http://www.aamn.org).

Tips for Success

To be a successful advanced practice nurse, you should

- be organized
- have good judgment
- be able to react quickly during emergencies
- have good time management skills
- be able to work well with others

about the proper foods to eat and how to stay healthy before they deliver their baby. They monitor the general health of expectant mothers to make sure that healthy babies will be delivered. Certified nurse-midwives deliver babies. Then they monitor and instruct mothers after the birth. They make sure that the mother and baby remain healthy.

Nurse anesthetists give patients medication for pain (anesthetics) or to help patients relax and sleep (sedatives). Some may work in dentists' offices. Nurse anesthetists may give anesthetics in a shot, or they may use special equipment and have the patient breathe in the anesthetic through a mask. During the operation, nurse anesthetists keep track of how deeply the patient is sleeping. If the patient starts to wake up during the operation, nurse anesthetists may give more anesthetic. They closely watch a patient's breathing and heartbeat during the whole operation. In emergencies, during surgery, or during the delivery of babies, they may have to make important decisions very quickly.

Clinical nurse specialists handle many physical and mental health problems of patients. They use patients' medical records, laboratory test results, and examinations to diagnose and treat illnesses. In addition to working directly with patients, clinical nurse specialists act as consultants (give professional advice), do research, and sometimes teach.

Advanced practice nurses are employed in community health centers, public health departments, hospitals and hospital clinics, school student health clinics, business and industry employee health departments, physicians' offices, Health Maintenance Organizations, nursing homes and hospices, home health agencies, Armed Forces and U.S. Department of Veterans Affairs facilities, and schools of nursing.

Education and Training

In high school, take math and science courses, including biology, chemistry, and physics. Health courses will also be helpful.

FOR MORE INFO

For information on a career as a nurse practitioner, contact
American Academy of Nurse Practitioners
PO Box 12846
Austin, TX 78711-2846
512-442-4262
admin@aanp.org
http://www.aanp.org

Visit the AACN Web site to access a list of member schools and to read the online pamphlet *Your Nursing Career: A Look at the Facts.*
American Association of Colleges of Nursing (AACN)
One Dupont Circle, NW, Suite 530
Washington, DC 20036-1135
202-463-6930
http://www.aacn.nche.edu

For information on nurses who care for patients before and after anesthesia is administered, contact
American Association of Nurse Anesthetists
222 South Prospect Avenue
Park Ridge, IL 60068-4001
847-692-7050
info@aana.com
http://www.aana.com

This organization is the largest and most widely known midwifery organization in the United States. The ACNM accredits midwifery training programs. For more information on the career and education of nurse-midwives, visit the ACNM Web site.

American College of Nurse-Midwives (ACNM)
8403 Colesville Road, Suite 1550
Silver Spring, MD 20910-6374
240-485-1800
http://www.acnm.org

For information on a career as a nurse anesthetist, contact
American Society of PeriAnesthesia Nurses
90 Frontage Road
Cherry Hill, NJ 08034-1424
877-737-9696
aspan@aspan.org
http://www.aspan.org

The following organization can provide information about all types of midwifery:
Midwives Alliance of North America
611 Pennsylvania Avenue, SE, #1700
Washington, DC 20003-4303
888-923-6262
info@mana.org
http://www.mana.org

For information on the career of clinical nurse specialist, contact
National Association of Clinical Nurse Specialists
100 North 20th Street, 4th Floor
Philadelphia, PA 19103-1443
215-320-3881
http://www.nacns.org

Discover Nursing provides information on nursing education and careers.
Discover Nursing
http://www.discovernursing.com

English and speech courses will teach you how to communicate well with patients.

If you are interested in becoming an advanced practice nurse you must first become a registered nurse. To become a registered nurse, you must complete high school. Then you must have one of three types of training: an associate's degree, a diploma program, or a bachelor's degree. After your registered nursing program, you must pass a state licensing exam. Advanced practice nurses can also obtain voluntary certification from various professional organizations.

After you become a registered nurse, there are a wide variety of requirements for the different types of advanced practice nurses. A master's degree is usually required, along with specific certification depending on the specialty. In the future, a Ph.D. will most likely be needed to work as an advanced practice nurse.

Earnings

Salaries (including overtime and on-call pay) vary greatly for advanced practice nurses. Salaries for nurse practitioners average about $84,000 a year. Certified nurse-midwives average about $90,000 a year. Nurse anesthetists average $147,000 a year. Clinical nurse specialists average $82,000 a year.

Outlook

In the next decade, there will be many jobs for advanced practice nurses. They have the training to perform some of the duties that doctors usually do. Because they receive lower salaries than doctors, more medical employers are hiring them to reduce costs. Hospitals and medical centers will rely more and more on advanced practice nurses in the future.

Biomedical Engineers

What Biomedical Engineers Do

Biomedical engineers are scientists who study how living things work. Some biomedical engineers do research in laboratories. They work with other scientists and medical doctors to learn more about all the different systems that keep people and animals alive. For example, they may study how the brain uses electrical energy or what chemicals help a plant cell make food. They use complex machines and instruments to take measurements and test new ideas. Biomedical engineers use computers to help figure out how living things will react to new circumstances.

Other biomedical engineers design machines, such as heart pacemakers or kidney dialysis machines, which help people with health problems. These *biomedical design engineers* use all they know about the human body to make artificial body parts that will work as well as the real ones. For example, artificial limbs that respond to the electrical impuls-

EXPLORING
- Visit http://web.me.com/cecil2/cwt/main_files/BME_Careers.pdf to read *Planning a Career in Biomedical Engineering*.
- Visit school and community libraries to find books and magazines about careers in medical technology.
- Join a hobby club devoted to chemistry, biology, radio equipment, or electronics.
- Talk to a biomedical engineer about his or her career.

Biomedical Industry Breakthrough

These are some of the devices developed by biomedical engineers:

- Artificial hearts and kidneys
- Artificial joints
- Automated medicine delivery systems
- Blood oxygenators
- Cardiac pacemakers
- Defibrillators
- Laser systems used in surgery
- Medical imaging systems (MRIs, ultrasound, etc.)
- Sensors that analyze blood chemistry

es of nerves can have fingers and toes that move exactly as they would in the natural limb.

Biomedical engineers also design machines and instruments that doctors can use to treat patients. For example, biomedical engineers have designed machines that bounce sound waves to give doctors a picture of what's inside a person's body. These machines are called ultrasonic imagery devices.

Some biomedical engineers are university teachers. They lecture in classrooms and show students how to use equipment and perform experiments in the laboratory. They also teach students how to perform research for their own projects.

Rehabilitation engineering is a new and growing specialty area of biomedical engineering. Its goal is to improve the quality of life for people with physical impairments. *Rehabilitation engineers* often work directly with the disabled person and modify equipment for individual use.

Biomedical engineers should have a broad interest in the sciences. They have to be able to use their knowledge to solve problems. Often this means working on one problem for a long time and paying attention to every detail of the results. Biomedical engineers also have to be good at working with others because they often are members of research teams. They should

Fame and Fortune: Willem Johan Kolff (1911–2009)

Willem Johan Kolff is considered the father of the development of artificial organs. He is best known for his invention of the artificial kidney. Each year, more than 200,000 people in the United States alone use a modern version of this machine to stay alive.

Kolff was born in Leiden, Holland. While attending medical school during World War II, he witnessed the death of a young man as a result of kidney failure. He was inspired to try to develop an artificial kidney machine to keep other people from dying. Few people thought he would be successful. Kolff built the machine himself out of sausage casings made of plastic and other materials he obtained from a factory and other sources. In 1945, the device he built was used for the first time to save the life of a woman who had kidney failure.

After World War II, Kolff came to the United States. He worked as a researcher and educator at the Cleveland Clinic in Ohio and the University of Utah. In addition to developing the artificial kidney, he designed the heart-lung machine that made it possible to conduct open-heart surgery and the first artificial heart (the Jarvik-7).

After his retirement at age 75, Kolff continued his research. He worked on developing the wearable artificial lung and other artificial organs. He received more than 120 international awards for his work during his lifetime, including the American Medical Association Scientific Achievement Award and the Albert Lasker Award for Clinical Medical Research.

Sources: *Los Angeles Times,* Academy of Achievement, TheScientist.com

also have creative personalities in order to be able to envision solutions to medical problems.

Education and Training

To become a biomedical engineer, you will have to earn a college degree. High school classes in science (including biology, chemistry, and physics) and mathematics will be a good basis for study in college.

Most biomedical engineers study an engineering specialty (such as mechanical or electronics engineering) for four years in a university and then go on for more years of advanced study in biomedical engineering. If you want to direct a research project or teach at the university level you will have to earn a doctorate. The minimum education necessary for any biomedical engineering position is a bachelor's degree, but it is getting harder to land a job these days with just a bachelor's degree. Typical courses in a biomedical engineering program include Engineering Analysis, Biomedical Image Processing, Biomechanics, Biomaterials, Biology for Bioengineers, Physics of Diagnostic Imaging, Tissue Engineering, Advanced Thermodynamics, Physiology for Engineers, Human Anatomy, and Bioethics.

Engineers whose work may affect the life, health, or safety of the public must be registered according to regulations in all 50 states and the District of Columbia.

Earnings

Biomedical engineers earned median annual salaries of $78,860 in 2009, according to the U.S. Department of Labor. New graduates receive starting salaries of about $49,000. Those with considerable experience and advanced education can earn more than $123,000 annually. Biomedical engineers with doctorates earn the highest salaries.

Salaries increase with experience. Engineers who work for private industry or in hospitals usually earn more than those who work for the government or for universities.

Outlook

Employment opportunities for biomedical engineers are expected to be excellent over the next decade. As people live longer, the demand for health care will increase. This means that

FOR MORE INFO

For information on medical and biological engineering, contact
American Institute for Medical and Biological Engineering
1701 K Street, NW, Suite 510
Washington, DC 20006-1520
202-496-9660
http://www.aimbe.org

For more information on careers in biomedical engineering, contact
American Society for Engineering Education
1818 N Street, NW, Suite 600
Washington, DC 20036-2479
202-331-3500
http://www.asee.org

To read *Planning a Career in Biomedical Engineering*, visit the society's Web site.
Biomedical Engineering Society
8201 Corporate Drive, Suite 1125
Landover, MD 20785-2224

301-459-1999
http://www.bmes.org

For information on high school programs that provide opportunities to learn about engineering, contact
Junior Engineering Technical Society
1420 King Street, Suite 405
Alexandria, VA 22314-2750
703-548-5387
info@jets.org
http://www.jets.org

Visit the following Web site for more information on educational programs and links to other biomedical engineering sites:
The Biomedical Engineering Network
http://www.bmenet.org

there will be more jobs for biomedical engineers in the future. As we understand more about how the human body operates, the more work there will be for engineers to help repair and replace body parts that are injured or damaged by disease. Those with advanced degrees will have the best chances of landing a good job.

Biomedical Equipment Technicians

What Biomedical Equipment Technicians Do

Today, physicians work with complex medical equipment such as heart-lung machines, artificial kidney machines, chemical analyzers, magnetic imaging devices, and even artificial hearts. It's easy to take these machines for granted. But what if one of the machines broke down? Surgery or treatments could be delayed. People could even die. To keep this from happening, medical employers hire *biomedical equipment technicians.* These skilled professionals inspect, maintain, repair, and install medical equipment. Biomedical equipment technicians are also known as *medical equipment repairers.*

One of the most important jobs biomedical equipment technicians (BETs) do is fix broken instruments. When a problem arises with equipment, technicians try to find the cause of the problem. If the problem is complicated, technicians might contact the manufacturer of the equipment for help.

Biomedical equipment technicians also install and test new equipment to make sure that it works properly. They often take apart and inspect pieces of equipment. They clean and oil moving parts. They test circuits, meters, and gauges to see that all are operating properly. They troubleshoot software and hardware problems on machinery with computer components. Technicians also keep records of equipment repairs, maintenance checks, and expenses.

Some technicians work directly with physicians, surgeons, nurses, and researchers. These technicians explain how certain

EXPLORING

- Visit http://www.aami.org/ student for more information about a career as a biomedical equipment technician.
- Read books and magazines about biomedical equipment repair. Most are geared for upper-level students and working technicians, but browsing through these publications will give you a general introduction to the field. Here are two book suggestions: *Biomedical Equipment Technicians*, by Roger Bowles (TSTC Publishing, 2008) and *Introduction to Biomedical Instrumentation: The Technology of Patient Care*, by Barbara Christe (Cambridge University Press, 2009).
- Join a club devoted to chemistry, biology, radio equipment, or electronics.
- Ask a teacher or counselor to arrange a visit to a local health care facility to interview a biomedical equipment technician. Ask the technician about his or her educational background, what a day on the job is like, and what new technologies are on the horizon.
- Volunteer at a local hospital. Naturally, you won't be asked to work with the biomedical equipment, but you will have the opportunity to see professionals on the job and experience being in the medical environment. Even if your duty is only to escort patients to their tests, you may gain a greater understanding of this work.

medical equipment works and how minor problems with the equipment can be solved.

Biomedical equipment technicians also work for medical instrument manufacturers. These technicians assist with the design and construction of new medical equipment. They also explain to hospital workers how to operate equipment.

DID YOU KNOW?

Where Biomedical Equipment Technicians Work

- Hospitals
- Physicians' offices
- Laboratories
- Research institutes
- Colleges and universities
- Independent service organizations
- Biomedical equipment manufacturers
- Government hospitals
- Military
- Self employment

Education and Training

If you are interested in becoming a BET, you must graduate from high school and complete a two-year training program. While in high school, you should take courses in chemistry, biology, and physics. Classes in English, mathematics, shop, and computer-aided design and drafting will also be helpful.

After high school, you can enter a two- or four-year program in medical electronics technology or biomedical engineering technology. In these programs, you will study anatomy, physiology, electrical and electronic fundamentals, computer science, chemistry, physics, and biomedical equipment design and construction. After

Tips for Success

To be a successful biomedical equipment technician, you should

- have excellent technical and mechanical skills
- be a good problem-solver
- be able to work well under pressure
- have good hand-eye coordination
- be attentive to detail
- have good communication skills
- be able to work as a member of a team
- be willing to continue to learn throughout your career

you graduate, you will receive on-the-job training and attend training courses offered by manufacturers.

Earnings

Biomedical equipment technicians earned mean annual salaries of $42,300 in 2009, according to the U.S. Department of Labor (DOL). New workers earn less than $25,750, while workers with experience and advanced education can earn more than $67,500. The DOL reports that BETs earned the following mean annual salaries by employer in 2009: general medical and surgical hospitals, $47,220; professional and commercial equipment and supplies merchant wholesalers, $44,940; and health and personal care stores, $36,220.

Outlook

Employment for biomedical equipment technicians is expected to be excellent during the next decade. The increasing use of electronic medical devices and other sophisticated biomedical equipment has created a need for technicians—especially those skilled in working with software and electronics. Medical employers have realized that keeping equipment in top condition saves money and keeps facilities running smoothly. As long as BETs can help hospitals and other medical institutions save money, the demand for them should remain strong.

FOR MORE INFO

For industry information, contact
American Society for Healthcare Engineering
155 North Wacker Drive, Suite 400
Chicago, IL 60606-1719
312-422-3800
ashe@aha.org
http://www.ashe.org

For information about careers and biomedical technology education programs, contact
Association for the Advancement of Medical Instrumentation
4301 North Fairfax Drive, Suite 301
Arlington, VA 22203-1633
703-525-4890
http://www.aami.org

For information about careers, contact
Medical Equipment and Technology Association
http://www.mymeta.org

Chiropractors

What Chiropractors Do

Chiropractors are trained primary health care providers, much like physicians. Chiropractors focus on wellness and disease prevention. They look at patients' symptoms. They also consider nutrition (the types of food people eat), work, stress levels, exercise habits, and posture (the manner in which we hold our bodies). Chiropractors treat people of all ages—from children to senior citizens. They most frequently treat conditions such as backache, disc problems (discs are parts of our spine), sciatica (pain caused by a problem with an injured disc), and whiplash (an injury to the neck caused

EXPLORING

- Visit http://www.acatoday.org/pdf/CareerKit.pdf to learn more about chiropractic careers and education.
- Learn to play an instrument, such as the piano, guitar, or violin, to improve your manual dexterity.
- Learning to give massages is another way to increase manual dexterity.
- Talk to a chiropractor about his or her career. Ask your counselor or health teacher to help arrange an interview.
- Take a tour of a chiropractic clinic.

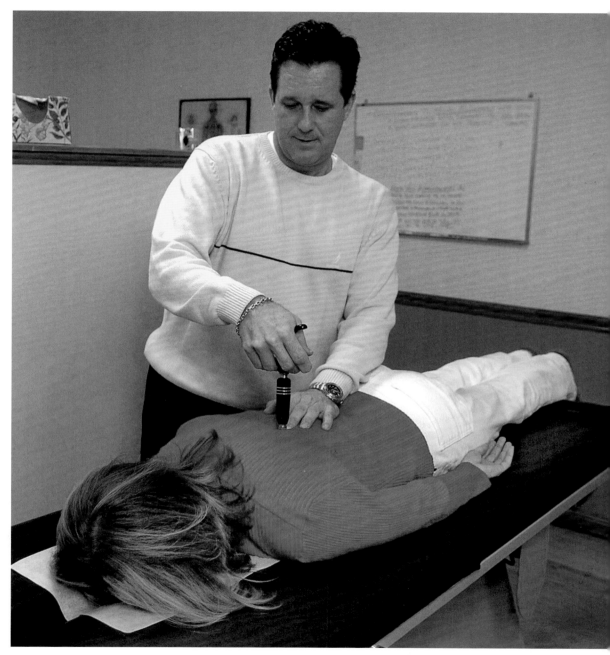

A chiropractor makes an adjustment to a patient's back. (C.W. McKeen, Syracuse Newspapers/The Image Works)

DID YOU KNOW?

- One of the earliest records of chiropractic-type medicine is in the *Chinese Kong Fou Document* written around 2700 B.C.
- Chiropractic became more recognized about 115 years ago when Daniel David Palmer (who is considered to be the founder of chiropractic) gave an "adjustment" that was felt to be a misplaced vertebra in the upper spine of a deaf janitor. The janitor then observed that his hearing improved.
- More than 22 million people in the United States seek chiropractic treatment each year.
- Approximately 44 percent of chiropractors are self employed.

Source: U.S. Department of Labor, American Chiropractic Association

by a sudden movement). They also care for people with headaches, respiratory problems, allergies, digestive trouble, high blood pressure, and many other common ailments. Some specialize in areas such as sports medicine or nutrition. Chiropractors do not use drugs or surgery. If they decide that a patient needs drugs or surgery, they send, or refer, the person to another medical professional. Chiropractors are also known as *doctors of chiropractic* and *chiropractic physicians.*

Doctors of chiropractic look for causes of disorders of the spine. They consider the spine and the nervous system to be extremely important to the health of the individual. Chiropractic teaches that problems in the spinal column (backbone) affect the nervous system and the body's natural defense systems. They believe spine problems are the underlying causes of many diseases.

On a patient's first visit, doctors of chiropractic meet with the patient and take a complete medical history before they begin treatment. They ask questions about the person's life to figure out the nature of the illness. Events in the patient's past that may seem unimportant may be very important to the chiropractor. These might include a car accident or sports injury. Then chiropractors do a careful physical examination. The examination may include laboratory tests and X-rays.

Once they have made a diagnosis, chiropractic physicians use a variety of ways to help make the person healthy again. The spinal adjustment is the treatment for which chiropractic is most known. During this procedure, patients usually lie on an adjustable table. Chiropractic physicians use their hands to work the spine. They apply pressure and use techniques of manipulation to help the affected areas of the spine. Chiropractic treatments must often be repeated over the course of several visits.

In addition to the spinal adjustment, chiropractic physicians may use drugless natural therapies, such as light, water, electrical stimulation, massage, heat, ultrasound, or biofeedback. Chiropractors also make suggestions about diet, rest, and exercise.

> **Tips for Alleviating Backpack Pain**
>
> - Make sure the backpack weighs no more than 5 to 10 percent of your body weight.
> - Make sure to place pointy or bulky objects away from the area that will rest on your back.
> - Wear both shoulder straps.
> - Use a backpack with padded, adjustable straps.
>
> Source: American Chiropractic Association

Education and Training

Science classes, such as biology, chemistry, physics, and psychology, will prepare you for medical courses in college. English, speech, drama, and debate can help you build your communication skills. Business, math, and computer science classes can help you get ready to run a private practice.

To become a doctor of chiropractic, you will have to study a minimum of six to eight years after high school. Most chiropractic colleges require at least two years of undergraduate study before you can enroll. Some require a bachelor's degree.

During the first two years of most chiropractic programs you will spend most of your time in the classroom or the laboratory. The last two years focus on courses in spinal adjustments. During this time, students also receive hands-on experience in outpatient clinics. After completing the six- or eight-year program, you will receive the degree of Doctor of Chiropractic (D.C.).

FOR MORE INFO

For general information and a career kit, contact
American Chiropractic Association
1701 Clarendon Boulevard
Arlington, VA 22209-2799
703-276-8800
http://www.amerchiro.org

For information on educational requirements and accredited colleges, contact
Council on Chiropractic Education
8049 North 85th Way
Scottsdale, AZ 85258-4321
480-443-8877
cce@cce-usa.org
http://www.cce-usa.org

For information on chiropractic medicine, contact
International Chiropractors Association
1110 North Glebe Road, Suite 650
Arlington, VA 22201-4795
800-423-4690
http://www.chiropractic.org

Earnings

The median annual income for chiropractic physicians was $67,650 in 2009, according to the U.S. Department of Labor. Those just starting out in the field make less than $32,750. Very experienced chiropractors earn more than $150,570.

Outlook

Employment for doctors of chiropractic is expected to be good during the next decade. The increasing number of older people—who often have more physical problems than younger people—is increasing demand for chiropractors. Many areas have a shortage of chiropractors. More insurance policies and Health Maintenance Organizations now pay for chiropractic services. While the demand for chiropractic is increasing, college enrollments are also growing. New chiropractors may find increasing competition for jobs. They will find it easiest to get a job in areas where few chiropractors practice.

Dental Hygienists

What Dental Hygienists Do

Have you ever had a cavity? If so, maybe you're not taking the advice of your dental hygienist and flossing and brushing your teeth enough. *Dental hygienists* help keep peoples' teeth clean. They work for dentists. Their main job is to remove plaque (bacteria that forms on teeth) and other deposits from the teeth, polish teeth, and massage gums. They also teach good oral health. They show patients how to select toothbrushes and use dental floss, what kinds of foods damage the teeth, and the effects of habits, such as smoking, on teeth. The main goal of a dental hygienist is to help patients prevent tooth and gum decay and keep a healthy mouth.

Hygienists who work for dentists in private practice may do more than clean teeth. They may take and develop X-rays, mix materials to fill cavities, sterilize instruments (get rid of harmful substances that may cause infection), assist in surgery, and keep charts of patients' teeth. Some hygienists have office duties as well, such as answering phone calls and making appointments for patients.

Not all hygienists work for dentists. Some work in schools where they clean and examine students' teeth and show them how to prevent tooth decay. They teach children and teens how to brush and floss teeth correctly and eat the right foods. They also keep records of the students' teeth and tell parents about any problems or need for more treatment.

Some dental hygienists work for local, state, or federal public health agencies. They clean the teeth of adults and children in

EXPLORING

- Read books about dental care and careers in the fields, such as *Opportunities in Dental Care Careers,* by Bonnie Kendall (McGraw-Hill, 2006).
- Visit Web sites to learn more about the field. Here are a few suggestions: Mouth Power Online (http://www.mouth-power.org), Visit the Dentist with Marty (http://www.ada.org/379.aspx), American Dental Hygienists' Association: Kids Stuff (http://www.adha.org/kidstuff), and American Dental Association: Dentistry Career Options (http://www.ada.org/3324.aspx).
- Ask your dental hygienist to show you the tools he or she uses. Hygienists will be happy to answer any questions you may have about their jobs.
- Practice good dental hygiene.
- Ask your dental hygienist to participate in an information interview about his or her career.
- Visit the Dr. Samuel D. Harris National Museum of Dentistry in Baltimore, Maryland, during your summer vacation or on a class field trip. If you can't make it to Baltimore, check out the museum's Web site, http://www.dentalmuseum.org.

public health clinics and other public facilities and educate patients in the proper care of teeth. Others work in the military.

Like all dental professionals, hygienists must be aware of federal, state, and local laws regarding hygiene practice. In particular, hygienists must know the types of infection control and protective gear that, by law, must be worn in the dental office to protect workers from infection. Dental hygienists, for example, must wear gloves, protective eyewear, and a mask during examinations. As with most health care workers, hygienists must be immunized (receive a shot) against contagious diseases

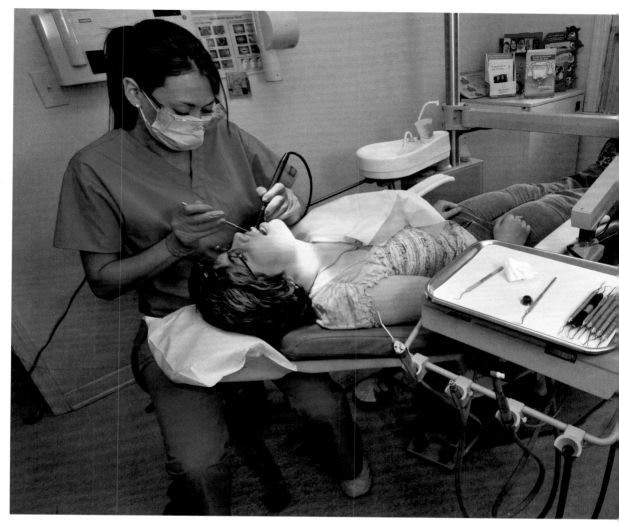

A dental hygienist cleans a patient's teeth. (Jessica Hill, AP Photo)

(those that can be passed from one person to another), such as hepatitis.

Education and Training

To become a dental hygienist, you must have a high school diploma. Recommended high school courses include biology,

DID YOU KNOW?

- Dental hygienists were initially known as "dental nurses," but dentists believed that this name suggested disease management, rather than preventive care, so their job title was changed.

- The first dental hygienists were trained by dentists themselves.
- In 1910, the first college classes in dental hygiene were offered by the Ohio College of Dental Surgery.

Tips for Success

To be a successful dental hygienist, you should

- be skilled in handling delicate instruments
- have a sensitive touch
- have good depth perception
- be punctual
- be organized
- have a pleasant personality
- be neat and clean

chemistry, mathematics, health, and speech. Then you must complete two or four years of college at an accredited dental hygiene school, and pass the national board exams for your state.

There are two types of dental hygiene programs. One is a four-year college program offering a bachelor's degree. The other is a two-year program leading to an associate's degree. More employers now require a four-year degree. During your education, you will study anatomy (the study of the structure of the human body), human physiology (the study of the systems of the human body), chemistry, pharmacology (the study of the effects of drugs, chemicals, and other substances on humans, animals, and plants), microbiology, nutrition, radiography, histology (the study of tissue structure), periodontology (the study of gum diseases), dental materials, clinical dental hygiene, and other sciences. You will also acquire hands-on experience.

FOR MORE INFO

The ADA has information on dental careers, education requirements, and dental student membership.
American Dental Association (ADA)
211 East Chicago Avenue
Chicago, IL 60611-2678
312-440-2500
http://www.ada.org

For information on admission requirements of U.S. and Canadian dental schools, contact

American Dental Education Association
1400 K Street, NW, Suite 1100
Washington, DC 20005-2415
202-289-7201
http://www.adea.org

For career information, contact
American Dental Hygienists' Association
444 North Michigan Avenue, Suite 3400
Chicago, IL 60611-3980
312-440-8900
mail@adha.net
http://www.adha.org

Earnings

Full-time dental hygienists earned median annual salaries of $67,340 in 2009, according to the U.S. Department of Labor. Beginning hygienists earn less than $44,900 a year. The most experienced hygienists in large cities can earn $92,860 or more.

Outlook

Employment opportunities for dental hygienists are expected to be excellent. In fact, the occupation of dental hygienist is one of the fastest-growing careers in the United States. Two trends are fueling job growth. As the population increases, more older people are able to keep their teeth as a result of better dental hygiene, and more employers are offering dental insurance. These trends will help create even more jobs for dental hygienists.

Dentists

What Dentists Do

Dentists help people have healthy teeth and gums. They do this by cleaning, filling, repairing, replacing, and straightening teeth. Dentists who are general practitioners do many kinds of dental work. They take X-rays, fill cavities, clean teeth, and pull diseased teeth. Dentists also talk to their patients about how they can prevent tooth and mouth problems. They give patients instructions on proper brushing, flossing, and diet. They must also be able to recognize problems that need the care of a dental specialist.

The American Dental Association recognizes nine dental specialties: dental public health, endodontics, oral and maxillofacial pathology, oral and maxillofacial radiology, oral and maxillofacial surgery, orthodontics and dentofacial orthopedics, pediatric dentistry, periodontics, and prosthodontics. Specialists devote their time and skills to specific dental problems. The following paragraphs describe the major specialties.

Public health dentists work through public health agencies to treat and educate the public about the importance of dental health and care. They must have excellent communication skills.

Endodontists specialize in diseases of the tooth pulp. The pulp consists of nerves, blood vessels, and other cells inside the tooth's root. The primary treatment they provide is the root canal. This treatment involves removal of the pulp from within the root canal, followed by filling of the root canal. Often, endodontic treatment is the only way to save a tooth that would

EXPLORING

- There are lots of hobbies that will develop strength and agility in your fingers and hands. Try sculpting, metalworking, model making, fine needlework, or any other activity where you need to do precise work with tiny parts.
- Learn all you can about dental care and practice good dental hygiene. Do the following: 1) Eat a balanced diet. Limit the snacks you eat, especially ones that contain sugar and starch. If you must snack, eat cheese, raw vegetables, plain yogurt, or fruit; 2) Brush your teeth twice a day with a fluoride toothpaste, and; 3) Floss between your teeth every day.
- Read books about dental care, dental history, and careers in the field. Here are two suggestions: *Opportunities in Dental Care Careers,* by Bonnie Kendall (McGraw-Hill, 2006) and *The Excruciating History of Dentistry: Toothsome Tales & Oral Oddities from Babylon to Braces,* by James Wynbrandt (St. Martin's Griffin, 2000).
- Visit Web sites to learn more about the field. Here are a few suggestions: Mouth Power Online (http://www.mouthpower.org), Visit the Dentist with Marty (http://www.ada.org/379.aspx), and American Dental Association: Dentistry Career Options (http://www.ada.org/3324.aspx).
- Consider volunteering in any medical environment to get experience in a health care setting.
- Talk to a dentist about his or her career.
- Observe a dentist during one of your appointments.
- Visit the Dr. Samuel D. Harris National Museum of Dentistry in Baltimore, Maryland, during your summer vacation or on a class field trip. If you can't make it to Baltimore, check out the museum's Web site, http://www.dentalmuseum.org.

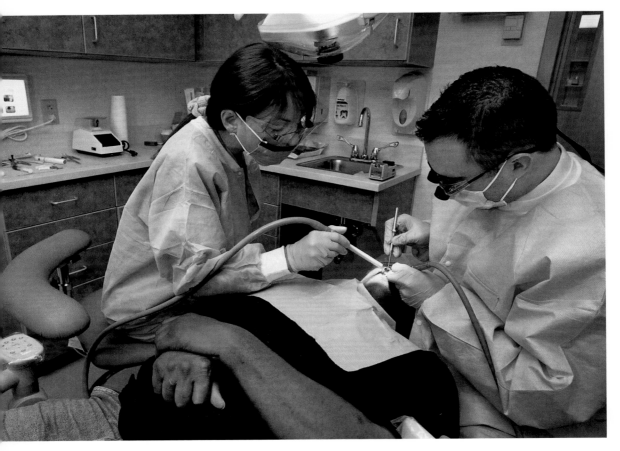

A dentist (right) *and dental assistant work on a patient.* (D. Lassman, *Syracuse Newspapers*/The Image Works)

otherwise have to be pulled. In some cases, endodontic surgery is required. The endodontist cuts through the gum surgically to expose the diseased root and surrounding bone. A portion of the root may be removed surgically.

Oral and maxillofacial pathologists examine and diagnose tumors and lesions (sores) of the mouth.

Oral and maxillofacial radiologists use radiation to produce and interpret images of the oral and maxillofacial region.

Oral and maxillofacial surgeons perform difficult tooth-pulling jobs. They remove tumors and fix broken jaws.

Orthodontists are dentists who have special training in the diagnosis, prevention, and treatment of dental and facial problems. The technical term for these types of problems is "malocclusion," which means "bad bite." Orthodontists design and apply corrective appliances, such as braces. These appliances slowly move patients' teeth, lips, and jaws into proper alignment. Extremely severe alignment problems may require orthodontists to perform surgery. Although orthodontists treat people of all ages, the majority of patients are teenagers. Most teens treated by orthodontists have to wear braces for one to three years. Some adults also see orthodontists to reduce tooth loss from periodontal (gum) disease, to treat symptoms of temporomandibular joint (TMJ) dysfunction, and to improve the appearance of teeth and jaws.

Pediatric dentists specialize in the care and treatment of children's teeth.

Periodontists treat diseased gums and other tissues that support the teeth.

Prosthodontists design, construct, and fit dental prosthetics.

About three out of four of dentists have their own private practices. Because many dentists work for themselves, they have to know about business matters, such as renting office space, hiring employees, running an office, keeping books, and stocking equipment. Other dentists work in research or teaching or hold managerial positions in dental schools. They also

DID YOU KNOW?

There have been many groundbreaking events in the history of dentistry. Here are just a few:

- 1498: The first toothbrush was crafted in China.
- 1728: Pierre Fauchard published *Treatises on the Teeth*. This publication helped dentistry become a respected medical discipline.
- 1840: The Baltimore College of Dental Surgery was founded. It was the first dental college in the world.
- 1844: Nitrous oxide anesthesia was invented.
- 1846: Ether was used as an anesthetic for the first time.
- 1990: The Food and Drug Administration approved the use of lasers in dental treatment.

Source: Dr. Samuel D. Harris National Museum of Dentistry

work for the government in the armed forces, public health services, hospitals, and clinics. Most dentists work 35 to 40 hours a week, including some time on weekends.

Education and Training

In high school, science and math courses are a good preparation for a career in dentistry. To become a dentist, you must complete three to four years of college-level predental education. Three out of four dental students have a bachelor's or master's degree. After college, you must go to an accredited dental school. Then you must pass the Dental Admissions Test. Training at a dental school takes at least four years. During this time, you will study basic sciences, including anatomy, biochemistry, microbiology, and physiology, as well as how to treat patients. After graduation, a dentist must take a state examination to receive a license to practice dentistry. Dentists who wish to enter a specialized field spend an additional two to four years

Helping Hands: Helping Battered Women Smile Again

Victims of domestic violence are sometimes so badly beaten that they lose their teeth. Some have even been shot by domestic partners, causing damage to the palate, teeth, and jaw. Victims often do not have dental insurance or money to repair this damage. The American Academy of Cosmetic Dentistry Charitable Foundation offers free dental care to those who have been abused via its Give Back a Smile Program. From July 2008 to June 2009, American Academy of Cosmetic Dentistry member-dentists donated $1.6 million in cosmetic and general dental treatments to 148 survivors of domestic abuse in 35 states. The foundation also has a Domestic Violence Intervention and Prevention Program that helps dentists identify and talk with suspected victims of domestic violence. Visit the foundation's Web site, http://www.aacd.com, for more information on these programs.

FOR MORE INFO

The ADA has information on dental careers, education requirements, and dental student membership.
American Dental Association (ADA)
211 East Chicago Avenue
Chicago, IL 60611-2678
312-440-2500
http://www.ada.org

For information on admission requirements of U.S. and Canadian dental schools, contact
American Dental Education Association
1400 K Street, NW, Suite 1100
Washington, DC 20005-2415
202-289-7201
http://www.adea.org

studying that specialty. Dental specialists can also receive board certification.

Earnings

According to the American Dental Association, the average income of self-employed dentists was about $207,210 in 2008. Some dentists earn less than $70,000. Specialists average $342,270 a year.

Outlook

Employment for dentists is expected to be good during the next decade. It is hard to get into dental school, though, because many people want to become dentists. It is important to earn high grades throughout your educational career so that you will be accepted to dental school.

Even stronger employment prospects are expected for dental specialists. Oral and maxillofacial pathologists and orthodontists, for instance, will be in great demand. Additionally, dentists who do cosmetic procedures such as fitting braces for adults will also be in demand.

Dietitians and Nutritionists

What Dietitians and Nutritionists Do

Did you know that there are professionals who advise people on eating habits and plan diets that will improve or maintain their health? They are known as *dietitians* and *nutritionists.* They work for themselves or for institutions such as hospitals, schools, restaurants, and hotels.

Registered dietitians (RDs) have completed strict training and testing requirements designed by the American Dietetic Association. They have a broad-based knowledge of foods, dietetics, and food service. They work in many settings.

Clinical dietitians plan and supervise the preparation of diets designed for patients. They work for hospitals and retirement homes. In many cases, patients cannot eat certain foods for medical reasons, such as diabetes or liver failure. Dietitians see that these patients receive nourishing meals. They work closely with doctors, who advise them regarding their patients' health and the foods that the patients cannot eat.

Community dietitians usually work for clinics, government health programs, social service agencies, or similar organizations. They counsel individuals or advise the members of certain groups about nutritional problems, proper eating, and sensible grocery shopping.

Certified clinical nutritionists have the same core educational and internship backgrounds as RDs but are specialists who have completed some postgraduate education that focuses on the biochemical and physiological aspects of nutrition science. Certified clinical nutritionists typically work in private practice for themselves, as part of a group of health care professionals, or for a doctor or doctors in private practice. They work with clients to correct imbalances in the clients' biochemistry and improve their physiological function.

Although most dietitians and nutritionists do some kind of teaching in the course of their work, *teaching dietitians and nutritionists* specialize in education. They usually work for hospitals, and they may teach full time or part time. Sometimes, teaching dietitians and nutritionists also perform other tasks, such as running a food-service operation, especially in small colleges.

Consultant dietitians and nutritionists work with schools, restaurants, grocery-store chains, manufacturers of food-ser-

EXPLORING

- Learn about the Food Pyramid by visiting http://www.mypyramid.gov.
- Visit the following Web sites to learn more about opportunities in the field: American Dietetic Association: Career Center (http://www.eatright.org/students/careers) and ExploreHealthCareers.org (http://explorehealthcareers.org).
- Read books about healthy diet and nutrition. Many cookbooks that feature healthy recipes

have sections on nutrition.
- Learn healthy ways to cook and bake. Plan and prepare meals for your family. Do your own grocery shopping, and learn to pick out the best produce, meats, fish, and other ingredients. Take cooking classes offered by your school and other organizations in your community.
- Ask a teacher or counselor to arrange an information interview with a dietitian or nutritionist.

Profile: Antoine-Laurent Lavoisier (1743–1794)

Antoine-Laurent Lavoisier was a French chemist who is known as the "father of nutrition and chemistry" for his work in these fields.

Lavoisier was born in 1743. As he grew into young adulthood, his father, a successful lawyer, wanted him to follow in his footsteps and practice law. Lavoisier obtained his law license, but soon realized that he was more interested in studying science—particularly geology. He also studied astronomy and botany and wrote an award-winning essay on how to light the dark streets of a big city at night. At the age of 25, Lavoisier was elected to the Royal Academy of Science.

Lavoisier began to study the way the body uses food energy, or calories. He also studied the relationship between heat production and the use of energy and the composition of air, among other studies.

Lavoisier had a strong interest in politics and social justice. His ideas and beliefs would be the cause of his downfall during the French Revolution. Based on false charges, he was arrested, tried, and executed.

Source: Chemical Heritage Foundation, Creighton University, Antoine-lavoisier.com

vice equipment, drug companies, and private companies of various kinds. Some consultants work with athletes and sports teams. They help improve athletes' performance and extend the length of their careers.

Research dietitians and nutritionists work for government organizations, universities, hospitals, drug companies, and manufacturers. They try to improve existing food products or find alternatives to unhealthy foods.

Education and Training

Recommended high school courses for those who want to become dietitians and nutritionists include biology, chemistry, health, family and consumer science, mathematics, and communications.

To become a registered dietitian, you must have a bachelor's degree in dietetics, food service systems management, foods and nutrition, or a related area. There are no specific educational requirements for nutritionists who are not dietitians, but most nutritionists have at least two years of college-level training in nutrition, food service, or another related subject. Many employers require nutritionists to have a bachelor's degree. If you want to teach, do research, or work in the field of public health, you will need one or more advanced degrees.

Tips for Success

To be a successful dietitian or nutritionist, you should

- be detail oriented
- enjoy math and science
- be able to work as a member of a team
- have good communication skills
- be willing to continue to learn throughout your career

Earnings

Dietitians and nutritionists earned median annual salaries of $52,150 in 2009, according to the U.S. Department of Labor. New workers earned less than $33,230. Very experienced dietitians and nutritionists earned more than $74,690. Dietitians and nutritionists who were employed at hospitals earned mean annual salaries of about $53,560.

Outlook

Employment of dietitians and nutritionists is expected to be good during the next decade. People are becoming more aware of the importance of nutrition, and they are asking experts for advice. The average age of the population is increasing. This will create a demand for nutritional counseling and planning in

FOR MORE INFO

The ADA is the single best source of information about careers in dietetics. Visit its Web site for educational and career information.

American Dietetic Association (ADA)
120 South Riverside Plaza, Suite 2000
Chicago, IL 60606-6995
800-877-1600
http://www.eatright.org

The goal of the ASN is to improve peoples' quality of life through the nutritional sciences.

American Society for Nutrition (ASN)
9650 Rockville Pike
Bethesda, MD 20814-3999
301-634-7050
http://www.asns.org

For information on certification, contact
International and American Associations of Clinical Nutritionists
15280 Addison Road, Suite 130
Addison, TX 75001-4551
972-407-9089
ddc@clinicalnutrition.com
http://www.iaacn.org

schools, residential care facilities, prisons, community health programs, and home health care agencies. Opportunities for dietitians will be best in contract providers of food services (outside companies that provide food services to organizations), in offices of physicians and other health practitioners, and in outpatient care centers. Hospital and nursing home dietitians may experience slower employment growth. Many hospitals and nursing homes are expected to hire outside companies to handle food-service operations.

Dietitians and nutritionists with advanced training and certification will have the best employment opportunities. Those with less than a bachelor's degree will have a tough time landing a job.

Emergency Medical Technicians

What Emergency Medical Technicians Do

Emergency medical technicians, or *EMTs,* drive in ambulances or fly in helicopters or fixed-wing aircraft to the scene of accidents or emergencies to care for ill or injured people.

EMTs decide what kind of medical help victims need. Then they treat them quickly. They may set broken bones or try to restart someone's heart. They must be able to stay calm and to calm others in a crisis.

The ambulances, helicopters, and fixed-wing aircraft EMTs ride in use two-way radios. At the scene of an emergency, EMTs may need to make radio contact with hospitals to ask for a

EXPLORING

- Read books and magazines about EMTs and first aid.
- High school health courses are a useful introduction to some of the concepts and terminology that EMTs use.
- Ask your health teacher to help arrange an information interview with an EMT.
- You may be able to take a first aid class or training in cardiopulmonary resuscitation. Organizations such as the Red Cross or a nearby hospital can provide information on local training courses.

Emergency medical technicians transport injured people from the scene of a crash. (Joe Brown, AP Photo)

physician's advice about treatment. On the way to the hospital, EMTs radio ahead so the emergency room is ready. They help carry the victims into the hospital and give the hospital staff as much information as they can about the patient's condition and the nature of the accident.

EMTs must keep their ambulances and aircraft in good order and make sure that they always have the equipment they need. This includes replacing used linens and blankets and replenishing supplies of drugs and oxygen.

EMTs work for hospitals, fire departments, police departments, private ambulance services, or other first-aid organizations. In fire departments, most EMTs work 50 hours a week; in hospitals, between 45 and 60 hours a week; and in private ambulance services, between 45 and 50 hours. Since people need emergency help at all hours, EMTs work nights, weekends, and holidays.

Successful EMTs have a desire to help people and are emotionally stable and clearheaded—especially during stressful situations. They must be confident, have good judgment, and be strong communicators. EMTs also must be in above-average physical condition and have good manual dexterity and motor coordination.

Education and Training

To be an EMT, you must first finish high school. You have to be at least 18 years old, and have a driver's license. High school courses in health, physics, chemistry, and mathematics are help-

Words to Learn

Amkus cutter a hand-held rescue device, similar to scissors, used to free trapped victims by cutting through metal

Amkus rams a hand-held rescue device used to free trapped victims by pushing or pulling obstructions, such as dashboard and seats, away from the victim

Amkus spreader a hand-held rescue device used to free trapped victims by pulling crumpled metal apart

backboard a long, flat, hard surface used to immobilize (stop it from moving) the spine in case of neck or spinal injury

defibrillator a machine with electrodes that is used to apply electric currents to heart muscles in order to shock the muscles into operation

endotracheal intubation the insertion of a tube into the trachea, or windpipe, to provide a passage for air, in case of obstruction

ful. A course in driver's education will be useful because EMTs need excellent driving skills. You need to know the roads and travel conditions in your area so you can drive to the scene of an emergency and to the hospital quickly and safely.

Many hospitals, colleges, and police and fire departments offer the basic EMT training course. In this course, you are taught how to respond to common emergencies such as bleeding, fractures (broken bones), airway obstruction, and cardiac arrest. You also learn how to use equipment such as stretchers, backboards, fracture kits, and oxygen delivery systems. The federal government requires all EMTs to pass this basic training course. All 50 states have some certification requirement. The National Registry of Emergency Medical Technicians offers certification to EMTs.

Earnings

EMTs who work for local government earn average salaries of about $36,780. Those employed by private ambulance companies earn $30,000, while those who work for general medical and surgical hospitals make about $33,390. Median annual earnings of EMTs and paramedics were $30,000 in 2009, ac-

DID YOU KNOW?

- More than 16 million patients are transported by ambulance each year.
- Approximately 210,700 EMTs and paramedics are employed in the United States.
- About 45 percent of EMTs and paramedics work for private ambulance services. Thirty percent work in local government for fire departments, emergency medical services, and public ambulance services. Twenty percent work in hospitals.

Sources: National Association of Emergency Medical Technicians, U.S. Department of Labor

FOR MORE INFO

This organization represents companies that provide emergency and non-emergency medical transportation services.

American Ambulance Association
8400 Westpark Drive, 2nd Floor
McLean, VA 22102-5116
800-523-4447
http://www.the-aaa.org

For information on EMT careers, contact
National Association of Emergency Medical Technicians
PO Box 1400

Clinton, MS 39060-1400
800-346-2368
info@naemt.org
http://www.naemt.org

For information on testing for EMT certification, contact
National Registry of Emergency Medical Technicians
Rocco V. Morando Building
6610 Busch Boulevard
PO Box 29233
Columbus, OH 43229-1740
614-888-4484
http://www.nremt.org

cording to the U.S. Department of Labor. Those just stating out in the field earned less than $19,360. Very experienced EMTs earned more than $51,460 a year.

Outlook

The employment outlook for EMTs should remain very good in larger communities. In smaller communities with fewer financial resources, there may not be as many jobs. The growing number of older people in the United States, who use emergency medical services more often than others, should increase the need for EMTs. Opportunities will be best for EMTs employed by private ambulance services.

Fitness Experts

What Fitness Experts Do

Fitness experts teach people how to exercise, eat right, and have a healthy lifestyle. Everyone has different fitness needs, so experts must design programs specially for each person's needs. Even when they teach classes, they must plan programs that will meet the needs of people at different levels of health and fitness. For example, they would create a more challenging exercise plan for a young person as opposed to one for an elderly person or someone who is recovering from surgery.

EXPLORING

- Visit a health club, park district, or YMCA/YWCA aerobics class to watch fitness trainers and aerobics instructors at work.
- Sign up for an aerobics class or train with a fitness trainer to learn firsthand what their jobs are like.
- Participate in school sports.
- Join local athletic clubs or start one yourself. Get a group of friends together to run or ride bikes at a regular time each week. Measure your fitness progress.
- Learn about nutrition and practice good eating habits.
- Ask your physical education teacher to arrange an information interview with a fitness expert.

There are two main types of fitness experts: *aerobics instructors* and *personal trainers.*

Aerobics instructors teach aerobic dance and aerobic step classes. The term *aerobic* refers to the body's need for oxygen during exercise. Aerobic exercise strengthens the heart and cardiovascular (blood) system.

Aerobics instructors sometimes teach special groups, such as the elderly or those with injuries or illnesses that affect their ability to exercise. They also teach those who are healthy, but who want to stay fit. Aerobics instructors use lively exercise routines set to music that can be changed to fit the needs of each individual class.

A typical class starts with warm-up exercises, or slow stretching movements that get the blood moving and increase flexibility. After the warm-up are about 30 minutes of nonstop activity to increase the heart rate. The class ends with a cool-down period of stretching and slower movements.

Personal trainers help health-conscious people with exercise, weight training, weight loss, diet, and medical rehabilitation programs. Personal trainers are sometimes called *fitness trainers.* During one training session, or over a period of several sessions, trainers teach their clients how to meet their health and fitness goals. They may train in the homes of their clients, their own studio spaces, or in health clubs.

Education and Training

If you're interested in health and fitness, you are probably already taking physical education classes and involved in sports activities. It's also important to take health classes and courses like family and consumer science, which offer lessons in diet and nutrition. Business courses can help you if you plan to run your own personal training service. Science courses such as biology, chemistry, and physiology are important because they will help you understand muscle groups, food and drug reactions, and other concerns of exercise science.

10 Summer Fitness Activities for Kids

After working hard in school all year, you might be tempted to hit the couch and play video games and watch TV once summer comes around. But it is important to stay active and avoid becoming a couch potato! By exercising, you'll feel healthier and get the chance to meet new friends. The American Council on Exercise recommends the following summer activities:

1. Soccer
2. Martial arts
3. Bike riding
4. Swimming
5. Basketball
6. Obstacle courses
7. Dancing
8. Board sports (surfing, skateboarding, etc.)
9. Jumping rope
10. Inline skating

Most fitness experts have a high school diploma. Many now have college degrees. A college major in either sports physiology or exercise physiology will help if you want to advance in the field.

Fitness experts must be certified in CPR. Most serious aerobics instructors and personal trainers become certified by professional associations.

Workshops and adult education courses at such places as the YMCA/YWCA will help you gain experience. Unpaid apprenticeships are a good way to get supervised experience before you teach classes on your own.

Earnings

Aerobics instructors are usually paid by the class, and start out at about $15 per class. Experienced aerobics instructors can earn up to $50 or $60 per class.

The IDEA Health and Fitness Association reports that the average hourly rate for personal trainers is $41. Hourly fees ranged from less than $20 to $70 or more. The U.S. Department of Labor reports that in 2009 the median annual salary for fitness trainers (including personal trainers) was $30,670.

Outlook

People in the United States are becoming more interested in health and fitness. As a result, fitness experts should have good opportunities in coming years. The number of elderly people in the United States is growing. This will create a need for aerobics instructors to work in retirement homes. Many large businesses

Fame & Fortune: Richard Simmons

You wouldn't recognize fitness personality Richard Simmons if you saw him back in his high school days in New Orleans. He weighed 268 pounds and didn't like how he looked or felt. He tried every type of fad diet imaginable, but finally realized that what it really took to lose weight was a healthy, balanced diet, exercise, and a lot of will power.

Simmons eventually lost some of the weight and moved to Los Angeles, but he was frustrated that he couldn't find a fitness club that catered to people like him—those who were not in perfect shape. He decided to create his own fitness plan for people of all ages. He began appearing on local television and radio shows to talk about his fitness plan and encourage people to lose weight by exercising and eating right.

In time, as a result of national media exposure (including a profile on the show *Real People* and eventually his own nationally syndicated series, *The Richard Simmons Show*), Simmons became a household name. Simmons has written more than 10 books about fitness and healthy eating. His 50 fitness videos have sold more than 20 million copies throughout the world.

Simmons has been successful because he is not in perfect shape (just like many people), he approaches fitness with a sense of humor, and he genuinely cares about people (he personally calls and e-mails his fans to encourage them). Additionally, his high-energy personality, combined with his trademark outfit (candy-striped shorts and tank top), allow him to stand out from other fitness experts.

Today, Richard Simmons continues to inspire people to lose weight and get healthy. You can learn more about Simmons by visiting http://www.richard simmons.com.

FOR MORE INFO

For information on careers, contact
Aerobics and Fitness Association of America
15250 Ventura Boulevard, Suite 200
Sherman Oaks, CA 91403-3215
877-968-7263
http://www.afaa.com

For more information about careers in fitness, contact
American Council on Exercise
4851 Paramount Drive
San Diego, CA 92123-1449

888-825-3636
support@acefitness.org
http://www.acefitness.org

For information about the fitness industry in general, and personal training specifically, contact
IDEA Health and Fitness Association
10455 Pacific Center Court
San Diego, CA 92121-4339
800-999-4332
contact@ideafit.com
http://www.ideafit.com

will also hire instructors to help keep their employees healthy. There is also more demand for personal trainers. People enjoy the convenience of being able to work out with a personal trainer at any time of the day, depending on their schedules. Some personal trainers are even beginning to work with clients in their own homes or at businesses. In the future, people will continue to be too busy with work and other responsibilities to exercise. This should ensure that fitness experts will continue to be needed.

Health Care Managers

What Health Care Managers Do

Health care managers direct the operation of health care organizations. These include hospitals, nursing homes, medical group practices, long-term care facilities, rehabilitation clinics, and health maintenance organizations. They oversee the building, equipment, services, staff, budgets, and relations with other organizations. Health care managers are also known as *health care executives.*

Health care managers organize and manage a wide variety of activities. They hire and supervise employees, figure budgets, set fees to be charged to patients, and establish billing methods. They buy supplies and equipment and set up ways to maintain the building and equipment. They make sure there are mail, phone, and laundry services for patients and staff. They make sure that their facility meets certain standards. Together with the medical staff and department heads, they develop training programs for staff.

Health care managers work closely with their facility's board of directors to develop plans and policies. Health care managers may also carry out large projects, such as fund-raising campaigns that help the facility change, update, and develop its services.

There are many types of health care organizations. In small facilities, health care managers usually handle all the management responsibilities and take a more direct role in daily operations. In large facilities, the *chief executive officer* in charge of managing the entire organization assigns duties to other managers.

Health care managers may be *generalists* (in charge of an entire facility) or *specialists* (in charge of specific clinical departments or services). Examples of areas within health care facilities that have specialized managers include clinical areas such as surgery, nursing, physical therapy, and psychiatry and administrative areas such as finance, security, maintenance, and housekeeping.

EXPLORING

- Visit the following Web site to learn more about a career as a health care manager: Make a Difference: Discover a Career in Healthcare Management! (http://www.healthmanagementcareers.org).
- Read books and magazines about health care management. Most are geared for upper-level students and working managers, but browsing through these publications will give you a general introduction to the field. Here are two book suggestions: *Introduction to Health Care Management,* by Sharon B. Buchbinder and Nancy H. Shanks (Jones & Bartlett Publishers, 2007) and *Careers in Healthcare Management: How to Find Your Path and Follow It,* by Cynthia Carter Haddock, Robert C. Chapman, and Robert A. McLean (Health Administration Press, 2002).

- Health care managers need to be leaders and talented speakers. To learn these skills you can participate in clubs of any kind as a leader or member. Join debate and speech clubs to develop speaking skills.
- When you get a little older, you can volunteer to work in a hospital or nursing home. This can help you learn about how health care facilities operate.
- Ask your counselor or health teacher to arrange an information interview with a health care manager.

Hospital administrators are generalists who work with the institution's governing board to develop long-range plans and policy. They set the overall direction of the organization. They deal with government regulations, fundraising campaigns, reimbursement, and community issues.

Department managers are responsible for staff, budgets, programs, and policies for their specific area. They may coordinate activities with other managers.

Group medical practice managers work closely with the physician owners to manage the practice. This allows physicians to spend time treating patients, not managing an office.

Office managers usually handle business matters for small group practices, while physicians make policy decisions. However, large medical group practices often hire a full-time health care administrator to manage the business operation and assign duties to assistants.

DID YOU KNOW?

Where Health Care Managers Work

Approximately 38 percent of health care managers work in hospitals, according to the U.S. Department of Labor. Managers also work in:

- Medical group practices
- Long-term care facilities
- Hospices
- Nursing homes
- Rehabilitation centers
- Psychiatric hospitals
- Health maintenance organizations (HMOs)
- Outpatient clinics
- Consulting firms
- Colleges and universities

Health maintenance organization managers have duties that are similar to managers in large group medical practices but may have larger staffs. They also may put more focus on preventive care. They develop plans and procedures that encourage patients to live healthier lives to keep them from getting sick in the first place.

To be a successful health care manager, you should have excellent communication skills. Much of this work involves dealing with people—from medical staff and department heads, to patients and their families, to community leaders and business-

Words to Learn

ambulatory care facility a facility that treats patients on an outpatient basis

HMO (Health Maintenance Organization) a prepaid managed care plan where members pay a fixed amount of money in exchange for most of their medical needs

hospice a facility that provides health care, especially pain control and emotional support, to terminally ill patients and their families

managed care a system for organizing many health care providers within a single organization to control health care costs

nursing home a facility that provides living quarters and care for persons unable to look after themselves, such as the elderly or chronically ill

PPO (Preferred Provider Organization) a managed care medical plan that contracts with doctors, hospitals, and other providers to obtain discounts for care; providers agree on a predetermined list of fees for all services

rehabilitation center a facility that uses therapy, education, and emotional support to help patients regain health to lead useful lives

es. You should be organized and able to make educated decisions quickly. It is also important to have a strong interest in the care of sick and injured patients. While caring about patients and staff, you also have to know how to manage budgets and save your employer money.

Education and Training

To prepare for this career, you should begin in high school by taking classes in business, mathematics, computer science, health, biology, chemistry, and social studies. After high school, you should go to college and take a wide range of courses, such as social sciences, economics, and business administration.

FOR MORE INFO

For industry information, contact
American College of Health Care Administrators
1321 Duke Street, Suite 400
Alexandria, VA 22314-3563
202-536-5120
http://www.achca.org

For general information about health care management, contact
American College of Healthcare Executives
One North Franklin Street, Suite 1700
Chicago, IL 60606-3529
312-424-2800
geninfo@ache.org
http://www.ache.org

For information about medical directors who work in long-term care services, contact
American Medical Directors Association
11000 Broken Land Parkway, Suite 400
Columbia, MD 21044-3532
800-876-2632
http://www.amda.com

For information about health care administration careers and accredited programs, contact
Association of University Programs in Health Administration
2000 North 14th Street, Suite 780

Arlington, VA 22201-2543
703-894-0940
aupha@aupha.org
http://www.aupha.org

For information about employment opportunities in ambulatory care management and medical group practices, contact
Medical Group Management Association
104 Inverness Terrace East
Englewood, CO 80112-5306
877-275-6462
http://www.mgma.org

For information about careers in health care office management, contact
Professional Association of Health Care Office Management
1576 Bella Cruz Drive, Suite 360
Lady Lake, FL 32159-8969
800-451-9311
http://www.pahcom.com

For detailed information about the career of health care manager, visit
Make a Difference: Discover a Career in Healthcare Management!
http://www.healthmanagement
careers.org

Many health care facilities hire only managers who have master's degrees in hospital or health services administration or a similar field. Some places hire managers who are physicians or registered nurses, or who have training in law or business along with health care experience.

Nursing home administrators must be licensed. Voluntary certification for health care managers is available from professional associations.

Earnings

Salaries of health care managers depend on the type of facility, location, the size of the staff, and the budget (the amount of money that is available to pay staff and operate the facility). Median annual salaries for health care managers were $81,850 in 2009, according to the U.S. Department of Labor. Managers just starting out in the field earn less than $49,750. Those with advanced education and considerable experience in the field can earn more than $140,000 annually. Health care managers who worked in hospitals had mean annual earnings of $96,660 in 2009, and those who worked in nursing care facilities earned $77,560.

Outlook

Employment in health care will be good during the next decade. The number of jobs in hospitals is declining, but there will still be many opportunities in this setting. Separate companies are being started to provide services such as outpatient surgery, alcohol and drug rehabilitation, or home health care. Many new openings should be available at these companies. There will also be many employment opportunities for managers in practitioners' offices and in home health care agencies. Managers with advanced education and experience will have the best chances of landing a job.

Home Health Care Aides

What Home Health Care Aides Do

Home health care aides care for people who live at home but are unable to care for themselves. Home health care aides usually assist the elderly or people with disabilities. They also work with children of parents with disabilities and people who are sick and need help for a short period of time. Aides help with such day-to-day tasks as laundry, shopping, and cooking. This assistance allows many people to stay at home instead of having to stay in nursing homes or other health care facilities. Job duties vary with the client's needs. For example, a home health care aide may help a client out of bed and into a wheelchair or change the clothes of patients who cannot do it by themselves. Aides often bathe clients, help with household chores, and prepare meals. For clients who have suffered an injury or are ill, home health care aides may help them do exercises, check vital signs (pulse, blood pressure, and temperature), or assist with medications. Home health care aides may also give bedridden people massages to keep their muscles strong. All of these health-related tasks are directed by a physician or registered nurse.

Home health care aides also provide emotional support. The aide may be the only person a client sees for long periods of time. The aide may cheer the person up and perhaps listen and give advice on personal problems. Often, an aide plays cards or other types of games with a client to keep the client occupied during the long hours at home.

Responsibilities vary and so does the length of time a home health care aide works with a client. Aides may help someone

EXPLORING

- Visit ExploreHealthCareers.org (http://explorehealthcareers.org) to learn more about opportunities in the field.
- Read books and magazines about health care and a career as a home health care aide. Here are two book suggestions: *Pocket Guide for the Home Care Aide*, 2d edition, by Barbara Stover Gingerich and Deborah Anne Ondeck (Jones & Bartlett Publishers, 2008) and *The Home Health Aide Handbook*, 2d edition, by Jetta Fuzy and William Leahy (Hart-

man Publishing Inc., 2005).
- Contact local agencies and programs that provide home care services and request information on their employment guidelines or training programs.
- Help a parent or older sister or brother care for an elderly relative or neighbor.
- Many communities have adopt-a-grandparent programs for children and teens.
- Ask a counselor or teacher to arrange an information interview with a home health care aide.

just released from the hospital on a daily basis for a few weeks or they may help an elderly person several times a week for an indefinite period.

To be a successful home health care aide, you should be in good physical shape. It takes strength, flexibility, and endurance to care for sick people. A positive and caring personality, as well as a willingness to serve others, are important qualities. At times you will have to be stern when dealing with uncooperative patients. At other times, you will need to be calm and understanding with those who are angry, confused, depressed, or in pain. You should genuinely care about and respect your patients. Cheerfulness and a sense of humor will help you establish a good relationship with a client, and a good relationship can make working with the client much easier. You must be willing to follow instructions and follow the health plan created for each patient. Doing this will help the patient get better faster.

Education and Training

There are no specific educational requirements for jobs in this field. Most employers prefer to hire those with a high school diploma and some experience working with the sick or elderly. Previous or additional course work in family and consumer science, cooking, sewing, and meal planning will be very helpful, as are general health and science courses. Volunteer work with sick and/or elderly people also is good experience. Many agencies provide several weeks of training to teach new aides how to bathe and care for patients and how to do basic housekeeping and cooking tasks.

DID YOU KNOW?

- Each year, approximately 7.6 million people receive care in their homes for chronic or terminal illnesses.
- There were 921,700 home health care aides employed in the United States in 2008.
- About 33 percent of home health care aides work part time.
- Approximately 8 percent of home health care aides are self employed.

Sources: National Association for Home Care and Hospice, U.S. Department of Labor

Home health care aides do not have to pass any tests or be licensed to work. But if a client's services are paid by Medicare (government health insurance), you need special training programs and you must pass a competency test. Voluntary certification is available from the National Association for Home Care and Hospice.

Earnings

Working hours and patient loads vary quite a bit. For many aides who begin as part-time employees, the starting salary usually is the minimum hourly wage ($7.25). For full-time aides with training or experience, earnings may be around $8 to $12

The Beginnings of Home Health

A typical household back in the 1800s often included an elderly parent or ill or injured relative. Families didn't have many of the modern conveniences we have today, so regular household chores could be impossible for someone weakened by illness or age. It was common for parents to move in with their grown children when they became unable to look after themselves. The needs of the elderly or sick person often took far more time and energy than the family could give. Running a household left little time for the family to care for the seriously ill.

Rural areas began to make "visiting nurses" available to check on patients who lived far from town and had no way to travel to doctor's offices. These nurses found that the needs of the patients went beyond medical care. Patients were thankful for the company of another person in their homes, someone to read their mail to them or run errands. The demand for this kind of home care increased and the profession of home care aides began to grow.

Advances in modern medicine have made it possible for many illnesses to be treated at home. The medical profession is also recognizing that people usually recover from illnesses better when they are treated in their homes.

an hour. The most experienced aides can earn more than $14 an hour.

Outlook

Employment opportunities for home health care aides will be excellent during the next decade. Government and private agencies are creating more programs to assist the elderly and people with disabilities. This means that the need for home health care aides will continue to grow. The number of people 70 years of age and older will increase in the next decade. Many of them will need at least some home care. Because of the work of home health care aides, hospitals and nursing homes can offer quality care to more people. This job is very demanding, both physically and emotionally. As a result, aides frequently change jobs and find other careers. This means that there are always job openings for home health care aides. In fact, this career is among those fields that will add the most positions during the next decade.

FOR MORE INFO

For information and statistics about the home health care industry, visit the association's Web site.
National Association for Home Care and Hospice
228 Seventh Street, SE
Washington, DC 20003-4306
202-547-7424
http://www.nahc.org

Medical Record Technicians

What Medical Record Technicians Do

Medical record technicians are in charge of putting together, organizing, and storing the medical records for patients. They use filing systems to keep track of this information. Filing systems can be located in filing cabinets and/or in computer files. Medical record technicians may also be known as *health information management technicians*.

Medical records are very complicated. Records show the patient's medical history, the results of physical examinations, and notes on any hospital stays. They list medications that have been prescribed, and any side effects the patient experienced (such as dizziness, nausea, sore throat, etc.). This information is later used by doctors, insurance companies, researchers, and others. For example, a doctor may want to know the last time he prescribed a certain medicine to you or what year you had your tonsillectomy. Researchers might want to see records of all babies born in a particular hospital in the past five years. Medical record technicians make sure this information is easy to find and well indexed. They might also create reports, using certain information from a large number of patient records.

All the information in the records is coded using a standard coding system. This system gives numbers to every disease, condition, and procedure. Using a code manual, special medical record technicians called *medical coders* enter this information into the filing system. Because the same code system is used by all health care professionals, a patient's medical records can be

EXPLORING

- Read books about health information management (HIM) such as *Essentials of Health Information Management: Principles and Practices,* by Michelle A. Green and Mary Jo Bowie (Delmar Cengage Learning, 2007). Although this book is geared toward upper-level students, it can give you a basic overview of typical job duties and skills for success in the field.
- Visit HealthInformation Careers.com (http://hicareers. org) to learn more about career options in the field.
- Visit http://www.hicareers. com/Health_Information_ 101/glossary.aspx for a glossary of HIM-related terms.
- Volunteer to be the secretary or treasurer for school clubs. These jobs will train you to keep careful notes and organize details.
- When you get to high school, you may be able to find summer, part-time, or volunteer work in a hospital or other health care facility. Sometimes such jobs are available in the medical records department for volunteers who can type or have clerical experience.
- Talk to a medical record technician about his or her career.

easily reviewed by caregivers across the country. Most medical facilities use computers to index medical records.

Cancer registrars maintain databases of cancer patients for physicians, public health organizations, and public health officials at all government levels. They code patient records and reports and conduct yearly follow-ups of patients listed in the registry. This allows them to track the effectiveness of treatments, survival and death rates, and other data.

Tips for Success

To be a successful medical record techni-cian, you should

- be very detail oriented and precise
- be familiar with medical terminol-ogy and codes
- be able to work rapidly as well as accurately
- be able to follow instructions
- be trustworthy because you will have access to other peoples' medi-cal information
- have good computer skills
- be willing to continue to learn throughout your career

Most medical record technicians work in hospitals. Some work in nursing homes, long-term care facilities, clinics, and doctors' offices. Others work for insurance companies, public health departments, home care providers, behavioral health facilities, consulting firms, rehabilitation centers, colleges and universities, information systems vendors, pharmaceutical companies, Internet-based health care companies, and health care research organizations.

Education and Training

High school classes in English, mathematics, and biology will help you prepare for this career.

Medical record technicians need a two-year college degree in health information management or a related field. More than 245 colleges and schools throughout the United States offer these degrees. Medical record science includes both classroom study and practical training, such as how to put statistics together or the different ways hospital departments keep records. There are also courses in ethics, since you must know when and how to give out information without violating the patient's right to privacy.

Earnings

Median annual earnings for medical record technicians were $31,290 in 2009, according to the U.S. Department of Labor

Words to Learn

abstracting taking information from a patient's records to create a short summary of their illness, treatment, and outcome

coding in medical records, assigning numbers for systematic classification

CPT (Common Procedural Terminology) the numerical classification system used in the medical records field to code procedures and treatments

diagnosis a word or phrase used by a physician to describe a patient's medical condition

DRG (Diagnosis-Related Grouping) a system used by Medicare and many insurance companies to classify medical patients' care and treatment

ICD (International Classification of Diseases) the numerical classification system used to code diagnoses

source-oriented chart order a system of organizing patient charts by grouping information into sections based on different health care departments, such as nursing, radiology, or attending physician

Terminal Digit Order a numerical filing method emphasizing the last two digits, which is the most effective use of filing space, as well as the most effective method to ensure patient privacy

transcribing making written copies of orally dictated material

(DOL). Salaries ranged from less than $20,850 to $51,510 or more. The DOL reports that medical record technicians earned the following mean annual salaries by employer in 2009: federal government, $45,120; general medical and surgical hospitals, $35,870; nursing care facilities, $33,100; outpatient care centers, $30,650; and offices of physicians, $28,4460. Experienced technicians in managerial positions can earn more than $60,000 a year.

Certified medical coders earned average salaries of $44,740 in 2009, according to the American Academy of Professional Coders. Those who were not certified earned $37,290.

FOR MORE INFO

For information on training and certi-fication, contact
American Academy of Professional Coders
2480 South 3850 West, Suite B
Salt Lake City, UT 84120-7208
800-626-2633
info@aapc.com
http://www.aapc.com

For information on earnings, careers in health information management, and accredited programs, contact
American Health Information Management Association
233 North Michigan Avenue, 21st Floor
Chicago, IL 60601-5809
312-233-1100

info@ahima.org
http://www.ahima.org

For information on a career as a cancer registrar, contact
National Cancer Registrars Association
1340 Braddock Place, Suite 203
Alexandria, VA 22314-1651
703-299-6640
info@ncra-usa.org
http://www.ncra-usa.org

For detailed information about careers in health information management, visit
HealthInformationCareers.com
http://himcareers.ahima.org

Outlook

Employment for medical record technicians is expected to be very good during the next decade. There should be many open-ings in the medical records field as the medical and insurance industries grow. Technicians will be needed to manage health records and convert paper files to electronic ones as stipulated by new laws. The strongest job growth will occur in nursing and residential care facilities, home health care services, and outpa-tient care centers. Growth will be less strong in hospitals, but there will still be many opportunities. Technicians with experi-ence in medical coding will have especially good job prospects.

Medical Secretaries

What Medical Secretaries Do

Medical secretaries do the administrative and clerical work in medical offices, hospitals, or private doctors' offices. They keep records, answer phone calls, order supplies, handle correspondence, bill patients, complete insurance forms, and transcribe dictation. Medical secretaries also keep financial records and handle other bookkeeping. They greet patients, make appointments, obtain medical histories, arrange hospital admissions, and schedule surgeries.

Medical secretaries play important roles in the health care field. They help physicians or medical scientists with reports, speeches, articles, and conference proceedings. Most medical secretaries need to be familiar with insurance rules, billing practices, and hospital or laboratory procedures.

Doctors rely on medical secretaries to control administrative operations. They spend a lot of time on the phone scheduling appointments and giving informa-

EXPLORING

- Read books about secretarial careers.
- Volunteer to be the secretary for school clubs.
- Offer to be the secretary for your class or run for a student government secretary position.
- Ask your school counselor to set up an information interview with a medical secretary, or arrange a tour of a medical facility so you can see medical secretaries in action.

Two medical secretaries confer about a patient's records. (Jeff Greenberg, The Image Works)

Deciphering Medical Terms

The words and terms that make up the language of medicine are tough to read and pronounce, and even harder to understand. Medical terms have changed over time, but most terms come from Latin or Greek words. Here's basically how medical terms are built.

Most medical terms can be broken down into one or more word parts: roots, prefixes, suffixes, and linking vowels. An example of a word with all of these parts is the term *electrocardiogram*. The prefix, *electro*, refers to electricity. The root, *card*, means heart. The suffix, *gram*, means a recording or picture. The vowels, *io*, connect the root to the suffix. So an electrocardiogram is a picture of the electrical impulses in the heart.

tion to callers. They organize and maintain paper and computer files, and handle correspondence for themselves and others. They might also type letters and handle travel arrangements. Medical secretaries operate fax machines and photocopiers. They use computers to run spreadsheet, word-processing, database-management, and desktop publishing programs.

Medical secretaries play a major role in large health organizations, such as clinical, research, and educational programs. Medical secretaries also are hired to fill positions as *medical transcriptionists.* Medical transcriptionists listen to recordings and transcribe, or type, reports of what the doctor said.

> **DID YOU KNOW?**
>
> **Where Medical Secretaries Work**
>
> - Private physicians' offices
> - Hospitals
> - Outpatient clinics
> - Emergency care facilities
> - Research laboratories
> - Large health organizations such as the Mayo Clinic
> - Colleges and universities

To be a successful medical secretary, you must use good judgment in dealing with private medical records. You must be confident when talking to people, both in person and on the telephone. You need a pleasant personality and a desire to help others. You should also be very organized and able to follow instructions.

Education and Training

Most employers require medical secretaries to have high school diplomas or the equivalent. You must be able to type between 60 and 90 words per minute. You must know medical terms and office procedures. You must be familiar with computers and be able to use medical software programs. Good writing, speaking, and basic math skills are important. Basic business courses will also be useful.

Some community colleges and vocational schools offer medical secretarial training, including medical transcription, computers, typing, accounting, filing, medical terminology, and medical office procedures. An associate's degree is sometimes required to work as a medical transcriptionist.

Medical secretaries can receive voluntary certification from the International Association of Administrative Professionals.

Earnings

Medical secretaries earned mean annual salaries of $30,190 in 2009, according to the U.S. Department of Labor. Starting salaries for medical secretaries are about $21,000 a year. Some medical secretaries earn more than $44,000 yearly.

Outlook

Employment for medical secretaries is expected to be good during the next decade. Organizations are demanding more from support personnel, including secretaries, according to the International Association of Administrative Professionals. Because they are asking more of secretaries, organizations are also increasing salaries. Medical secretaries with formal medical secretarial training will have the best employment prospects.

Medical Technologists

What Medical Technologists Do

Medical technologists do laboratory tests to help physicians find, diagnose, and treat diseases. They are usually supervised by a *pathologist*, a medical doctor who specializes in finding the causes and characteristics of diseases.

Technologists stain and mount slides with samples and examine them under a microscope. This allows them to see disease or damage to the cells. Medical technologists perform blood counts and skin tests. They do blood tests, including tests to determine blood types. They maintain blood supplies to be used for transfusions (the transfer of blood from one person to another). Technologists also use microscopes to examine body fluids and tissue samples for bacteria, viruses, or other organisms. They test samples of blood and urine to find out if drugs, chemicals, or poisons are present.

Technologists prepare samples of tissue and bone for pathologists to examine. The samples are preserved in a variety of ways, including freezing. Many times an abnormal growth is sent to a laboratory while a patient is in surgery. The technologist tests the growth to see if it is cancerous. The test results help the surgeon decide how to proceed with the operation. Technologists also help pathologists determine the cause of death and preserve organs for later examination. Some medical technologists do research on new drugs. Others help to improve methods of laboratory testing.

EXPLORING

- Visit the following Web resources to learn more about opportunities in the field: *Careers in Pathology and Medical Laboratory Science* (http://www.ascp.org/pdf/CareerBooklet.aspx) and ExploreHealthCareers.org (http://explorehealthcareers.org).
- Join a science club at school.
- Learn how to use a microscope. Learn how to prepare samples on slides for viewing under a microscope.
- Work on science projects and experiments that involve lab work and chemistry. Become familiar with lab equipment and procedures. Ask for help from your science teacher.
- Ask your science or health teacher to arrange a tour of a medical laboratory.
- Talk to a medical technologist about his or her job. Ask the following questions: What made you want to enter this career? What are your typical hours? What kinds of tools and equipment do you use to do your job? What do you like most and least about your career? How did you train for the field? What advice would you give to someone who is interested in the career?

Some medical laboratory technologists specialize. Those who work in the hematology department analyze cells from blood and bone marrow. *Hematology technologists* diagnose and monitor patients with anemia and leukemia and other blood infections. *Serology technologists* do tests for syphilis, rheumatoid arthritis, and lupus. *Cytotechnologists* study cells under microscopes, searching for cell abnormalities such as changes in color, shape, or size that might indicate the presence of disease. *Microbiology technologists* identify bacteria, viruses, and fungi that cause disease. *Immunology technologists* study elements of

Words to Learn

blood bank the lab area where technicians draw blood from donors; technicians also separate, identify, and match its components.

cytology the study of cells

hematology the lab area that counts, describes, and identifies cells in blood and other body fluids

histology the study of the structure and function of normal and abnormal tissue.

immunology the branch of medicine dealing with the body's ability to cope with infections

pathology the study of the nature of disease, its structure, and the changes produced by disease

virology the study of viruses and viral diseases

the human immune system. *Clinical chemistry technologists* test patients' body fluids to identify infections, kidney or liver disease, and pregnancy by analyzing the presence of certain chemicals. *Molecular pathology technologists* conduct nucleic acid and protein testing on cell samples to help identify and predict the development of diseases such as cancer and create effective drugs to treat them.

Medical technologists must pay close attention to detail. They must be good at observing and analyzing. They should be able to follow instructions. They must stay calm under pressure. Other essential characteristics are manual dexterity, good eyesight (with or without glasses), strong communication skills, and the ability to work as a member of a team.

Education and Training

High school courses in mathematics, biology, chemistry, physics, and computer science are important for a career in medical technology.

DID YOU KNOW?

Where Medical Technologists Work

- Hospitals
- Laboratories
- Clinics
- Public health agencies
- Physicians' offices
- Drug companies
- Research institutions
- Colleges and universities
- U.S. military

You must earn a bachelor's degree in medical technology or one of the life sciences for most jobs. Typical courses include those in biological sciences, microbiology, chemistry, mathematics, statistics, and specialized courses in laboratory practices and safety. Some technologists earn master's degrees or doctorates in this field. They may get jobs in teaching and research.

Some states require medical technologists to be licensed or registered. Voluntary certification is available from several professional associations.

Earnings

Medical and clinical laboratory technologists earned median annual salaries of $55,140 in 2009, according to the U.S. Department of Labor (DOL). Salaries ranged from less than $37,540 to more than $75,960. The DOL reports the following mean annual salaries for medical and clinical laboratory technologists by employer in 2009: federal government, $62,860; general medical and surgical hospitals, $56,400; medical and diagnostic laboratories, $54,960; offices of physicians, $51,550, and colleges and universities, $52,220. Medical technologists who are certified earn higher salaries than those who do not have certification.

Outlook

Employment for medical technologists is expected to be excellent during the next decade. As the U.S. population grows and more new tests are developed, there will be a strong demand for

FOR MORE INFO

For information on education and careers, contact

American Association for Clinical Chemistry
1850 K Street, NW, Suite 625
Washington, DC 20006-2215
800-892-1400
custserv@aacc.org
http://www.aacc.org

For information on certification, contact

American Association of Bioanalysts
906 Olive Street, Suite 1200
St. Louis, MO 63101-1448
314-241-1445
http://www.aab.org

For career and certification information, contact

American Medical Technologists
10700 West Higgins Road, Suite 150
Rosemont, IL 60018-3722
847-823-5169
http://www.amt1.com

For information about clinical laboratory careers, contact

American Society for Clinical Laboratory Science
6701 Democracy Boulevard, Suite 300
Bethesda, MD 20817-1574
301-657-2768
ascls@ascls.org
http://www.ascls.org

For information on certification and careers, contact

American Society for Clinical Pathology
33 West Monroe, Suite 1600
Chicago, IL 60603-5308
312-541-4999
http://www.ascp.org

For information on accredited schools and the accrediting process, contact

National Accrediting Agency for Clinical Laboratory Sciences
5600 North River Road, Suite 720
Rosemont, IL 60018-5119
847-939-3597
info@naacls.org
http://www.naacls.org

medical technologists. The greatest need will be in medical and diagnostic laboratories, physicians' offices, and all other ambulatory health care services.

Nurse Assistants

What Nurse Assistants Do

Nurse assistants take care of the personal needs of patients. They work in hospitals, nursing homes, and other facilities. Their duties vary according to the place they work and the kind of patients they care for. In general, they help move patients, assist in patients' exercise and nutrition needs, and oversee patients' personal hygiene. They are supervised by nurses. Nurse assistants are also called *nurse aides, orderlies, hospital attendants, direct care workers, care assistants, hospice assistants, geriatric nurse assistants, home care assistants, caregivers, resident assistants, personal care assistants, restorative aides,* and *patient care assistants.*

Nurse assistants answer patients' message bells. They serve and feed patients' meals. They make beds; help patients to dress, undress, and bathe; give massages; take temperatures; bring and empty bedpans; help patients get out of bed and walk; and take them places in wheelchairs or on stretchers. Some aspects of the job are difficult and unpleasant, such as assisting a resident with elimination and cleaning up after a patient who has vomited.

EXPLORING

- Read books and magazines about health care.
- Offer to care for a sick grandparent or neighbor. You can help an adult run errands, do laundry, or prepare meals.
- Learn about first aid, nutrition, exercise, and massage.
- Ask a teacher or counselor to arrange an information interview with a nurse assistant.

A nurse assistant (right) *and a nurse lift a patient from his bed to his wheelchair.* (Rob Goebel, *The Indianapolis Star*/AP Photo)

Nurse assistants in nursing homes and long-term health care facilities usually have much more contact with the patients than other members of the staff, and they often develop positive ongoing relationships with the people under their care.

Nurse assistants must sometimes work with disturbed, confused, anxious, or even violent patients. These experiences can be emotionally exhausting for the assistants, who must always act professionally and maintain a calm, patient, and sympathetic manner. Other important skills for nurse assistants include having a cheerful personality, being punctual, having the ability to follow instructions, and a willingness to perform often repetitive tasks.

Education and Training

Most employers prefer to hire people with a high school diploma. Some high schools work with local hospitals or nursing homes to offer health care courses. These classes may include body mechanics, infection control, and resident/patient rights. English and speech classes will help develop your communication skills. Science courses, such as biology and anatomy, and family and consumer science, health, and nutrition classes are also helpful. Learning a foreign language might help you provide extra special care to patients who do not speak English as a first language. One recommended language to learn is Spanish.

Most nursing homes and hospitals offer on-the-job training, which can last anywhere from two weeks to three months. There are training courses available at community colleges and vocational schools that teach basic nursing skills and prepare you for the state certification exam.

Many people work as nurse assistants as they pursue other medical professions such as a premedical or nursing program.

DID YOU KNOW?

Where Nurse Assistants Work

- Nursing homes
- Hospitals
- Retirement centers
- Homes for people with disabilities
- Private homes
- Residential care facilities
- Mental health facilities
- Drug and alcohol rehabilitation centers
- Home care settings

Earnings

Salaries for nurse assistants are not high, but all assistants earn at least minimum wage ($7.25/hour). Median hourly earnings for nurse assistants were $11.56 in 2009, according to the U.S. Department of Labor. Very experienced nurse assistants can earn more than $33,000. Nursing homes pay nurse assistants mean annual salaries of about $24,000 a year.

Mean wages in hospitals are higher—about $26,000.

Outlook

Job prospects for nurse assistants will be healthy during the next decade. As our population grows and ages, geriatric nurse assistants will be needed to care for elderly patients. Though fewer aides will be hired by hospitals, many more will be needed by long-term health care facilities and nursing homes. Many nurse assistants leave the profession because the pay is low and the work is demanding. Others consider work as a nurse assistant a stepping-stone on the path to employment as a nurse or physician. As a result, there will be many employment opportunities.

DID YOU KNOW?

- Approximately 41 percent of nurse assistants work in nursing and residential care facilities. Twenty-nine percent work in hospitals.
- Most full-time nurse assistants work 40 hours per week.
- Twenty-four percent of nurse assistants work part-time—8 percent higher than the average for all workers.

Source: U.S. Department of Labor, National Network of Career Nursing Assistants

FOR MORE INFO

For information and statistics on the home health care industry, visit the association's Web site.
National Association for Home Care and Hospice
228 Seventh Street, SE
Washington, DC 20003-4306
202-547-7424
http://www.nahc.org

For additional information on nurse assistant careers and training, contact
National Network of Career Nursing Assistants
cnajeni@aol.com
http://www.cna-network.org

Nurses

What Nurses Do

Nurses care for people who are sick, injured, or mentally ill. Nurses have a wide variety of duties. They comfort and assist patients, give treatments and medication, record patients' progress, and prepare equipment. Depending on their training, nurses also assist physicians and surgeons in medical procedures and supervise or teach other nursing staff. Nurses can specialize in many different areas.

General duty nurses work as part of a health care team. The team determines a patient's condition and decides on a health care plan. Nurses take patients' blood pressure, temperature, and pulse. They give medications. They note the patient's condition and symptoms. They change dressings, get patients ready for surgery, and complete any other duties that require skill and an understanding of the patient's needs.

Surgical nurses assist surgeons during operations. *Maternity nurses* help in the delivery room and take care of newborns in the nursery. They teach mothers how to feed and care for their babies. *Private duty nurses* work in hospitals and in patients' homes. They are employed by the patient or the patient's family, and they work under the supervision of the patient's physician. *Occupational health nurses* work in plants or factories. They give first aid treatment in emergencies. They also offer preventive and educational nursing services. *School nurses* supervise the student clinic, treat minor ailments and injuries, and give general health advice. *Hospice nurses* work with the terminally ill. They may treat patients in hospitals or hospice facilities, but often travel to patients' homes to offer treatment.

EXPLORING

- Check out the following online resources: Discover Nursing (http://www.discovernursing.com) and Your Nursing Career: A Look at the Facts (http://www.aacn.nche.edu/Education/nurse_ed/career.htm).
- Read books about famous nurses, such as Clara Barton, Elizabeth Fry, Edith Cavell, and Florence Nightingale. You should also read books about nursing careers. Here are a few suggestions: *A Career in Nursing: Is It Right For Me?,* by Janet Katz (Mosby, 2007), *Opportunities in Nursing Careers,* 2d edition, by Keville Frederickson (McGraw-Hill, 2003), and *Your Career in*

Nursing: Manage Your Future in the Changing World of Health-care, 5th edition, by Annette Vallano (Kaplan Publishing, 2008). These books are geared toward older students and new nurses, but browsing them can give you a good general introduction to the field.
- Talk to your school nurse or local public health nurse about their careers.
- Visit your local hospital and other health care settings to observe different work environments for nurses.
- Volunteer to work at a hospital, community health center, or even a local Red Cross chapter.

Licensed practical nurses, sometimes called *licensed vocational nurses,* perform the basic duties of nursing, including general patient care, the giving of medication, and clerical duties. They work under the supervision of registered nurses (R.N.s) and physicians. *Advanced practice nurses* are nurses who have received training beyond the R.N. level. (See the article "Advanced Practice Nurses" for more information on these nursing specialists.)

To be a successful nurse, you should enjoy working with and helping people. Patience, compassion, and calmness are qualities needed by anyone working in this career. In addition, you must

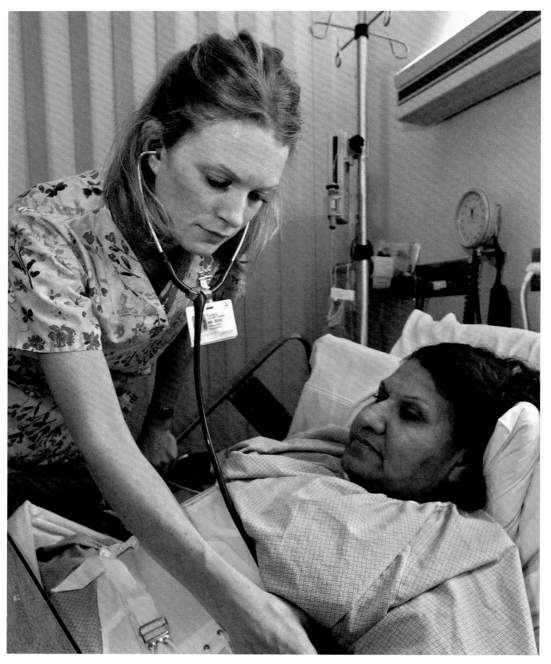

A registered nurse uses a stethoscope to examine a patient. (Rich Pedroncelli, AP Photo)

be able to give directions, follow instructions when necessary, and work as part of a health care team. Other key traits for nurses include excellent communication skills and the ability to work under pressure and multitask.

Education and Training

High school classes in biology, chemistry, health, mathematics, and social science provide a good background for nursing. English and speech courses will help you to develop your communication skills.

Licensed practical nurses usually complete a one-year educational program after high school. To become a registered nurse, you must choose one of three training programs. An associate's degree program is a two-year program offered at a community or junior college. A diploma program is a three-year program offered at hospitals and nursing schools. Bachelor's degree programs are four- or five-year programs offered at colleges and universities. You must earn a bachelor's degree in nursing for most supervisory and administrative positions, for jobs in public health agencies, and for admission to graduate nursing programs. A master's degree is usually necessary to prepare for a nursing specialty or to teach. For some specialties, such as nursing research, you must earn a Ph.D.

All states require nurses to pass an examination to be licensed. Voluntary certification is available from a wide range of nursing associations.

DID YOU KNOW?

Where Nurses Work

- Hospitals
- Physicians' offices
- Clinics
- Nursing homes and hospices
- Home health agencies
- Community health centers
- Public health departments
- School student health clinics
- Business and industry employee health departments
- Health Maintenance Organizations
- Camps
- U.S. military
- Government agencies (such as the U.S. Department of Veterans Affairs, Centers for Disease Control, etc.)
- Colleges and universities

Earnings

Registered nurses earned median annual salaries of $63,750 in 2009, according to the U.S. Department of Labor (DOL). Salaries ranged from less than $43,970 to more than $93,700. The DOL reports the following mean annual salaries for registered nurses by employer in 2009: federal government, $77,830; general medical and surgical hospitals, $67,740; offices of physicians, $67,290; outpatient care centers, $65,690; home health care services, $63,300; and nursing care facilities, $59,320. Salaries for licensed practical nurses ranged from less than $28,890 to $55,090 or more in 2009, according to the DOL. Nurses who are certified earn higher salaries than those who do not have certification.

Outlook

Nursing is the largest of all the health care occupations. As a result, there are many jobs available. Employment opportunities for registered nurses should be excellent during the next decade. The following employers (in descending order) will offer the most jobs: offices of physicians; home health services; nursing care facilities; employment services; and general medical and surgical hospitals, public and private.

Employment for licensed practical nurses is expected to be very good during the next 10 years. The most new jobs will be available in home health care services and nursing care facilities. Fewer job opportunities will be available at hospitals.

Nurses with advanced education, experience, and certification will have the best employment prospects. There are short-

FOR MORE INFO

Visit the AACN Web site to access a list of member schools and to read the online pamphlet *Your Nursing Career: A Look at the Facts.*

American Association of Colleges of Nursing (AACN)
One Dupont Circle, NW, Suite 530
Washington, DC 20036-1135
202-463-6930
http://www.aacn.nche.edu

For information about opportunities as an R.N., contact the following organizations:

American Nurses Association
8515 Georgia Avenue, Suite 400
Silver Spring, MD 20910-3492
800-274-4262
http://www.nursingworld.org

American Society of Registered Nurses
1001 Bridgeway, Suite 233
Sausalito, CA 94965-2104
415-331-2700
office@asrn.org
http://www.asrn.org

For information on a career as a licensed practical nurse, contact the following organizations:

National Association for Practical Nurse Education and Service
1940 Duke Street, Suite 200
Alexandria, VA 22314-3452
703-933-1003
http://www.napnes.org

National Federation of Licensed Practical Nurses
605 Poole Drive
Garner, NC 27529-5203
919-779-0046
http://www.nflpn.org

For information about state-approved programs and information on nursing, contact the following organizations:

National League for Nursing
61 Broadway, 33rd Floor
New York, NY 10006-2701
212-363-5555
http://www.nln.org

National Organization for Associate Degree Nursing
7794 Grow Drive
Pensacola, FL 32514-7072
850-484-6948
http://www.noadn.org

ages of nurses in rural areas and inner cities. Nurses who are willing to work in these settings will have especially good job prospects.

Orthotists and Prosthetists

What Orthotists and Prosthetists Do

Prosthetists make artificial limbs for patients who have lost limbs. *Orthotists* make braces to support weak limbs or help correct a physical problem, such as a deformed spine.

Great advances have been made in the design and manufacture of orthotic and prosthetic devices. Patients with high-tech, custom-fabricated and -fitted prosthetics can run races, swim, walk up stairs comfortably, and otherwise participate in daily life. Orthoses are now even made with funky colors or designs based on the tastes of the wearer.

Physicians refer patients to an orthotist or a prosthetist. Orthotists and prosthetists first examine their patients to determine what type of device is needed. A prosthetist uses tapes, rulers, or electronic devices to measure limbs or stumps carefully. Orthotists also take detailed measurements for braces. Today, computer-aided design/computer-aided manufacturing (CAD/CAM) technology is increasingly being used to measure, design, and manufacture orthotic and prosthetic devices. The device must fit the patient well so that it will work properly without causing irritation. Orthotists and prosthetists always try to design the most comfortable, useful, and natural-looking device possible. Each device is specially designed to match an individual's body. Orthotists and prosthetists are often assisted by *orthotic and prosthetic technicians.*

Materials used in the construction of orthoses and prostheses include wood, foam, plastics, fabric, steel, aluminum, fiberglass, and leather, as well as newer, composite materials, such as car-

EXPLORING

- Read books and magazines about orthotics and prosthetics.
- Visit the following Web site for information about education and careers in the field: Orthotics & Prosthetics: Make a Career of Making a Difference Everyday! (http://www.opcareers.org).
- Visit http://www.ispo.ca/lexicon for definitions of common terms used in orthotics and prosthetics.
- Teachers and counselors may be able to arrange for you to visit a hospital, clinic, or rehabilitation center so that you can observe orthotists and prosthetists at work.

- Read all you can about science, especially physics and engineering.
- Try to invent machines or tools of all kinds.
- Read about robotics.
- Ask a counselor or teacher to arrange an information interview with an orthotist or prosthetist. Ask the following questions: What made you want to enter this career? What are your typical hours? What type of tools do you use to do your job? What do you like most and least about your job? How did you train for the field? What advice would you give to someone who is interested in the career?

bon-graphite, titanium, and Kevlar. Orthotists and prosthetists use hand and power tools, such as saws, drills, and sewing machines, to skillfully manipulate these materials into the desired designs. They may glue, bolt, weld, sew, and rivet parts together or take advantage of advanced thermoforming techniques (techniques using heat) to mold and form parts. Straps or Velcro may be added to help customize the fit. Some orthoses and prostheses are now made by automated machinery. CAD/CAM tech-

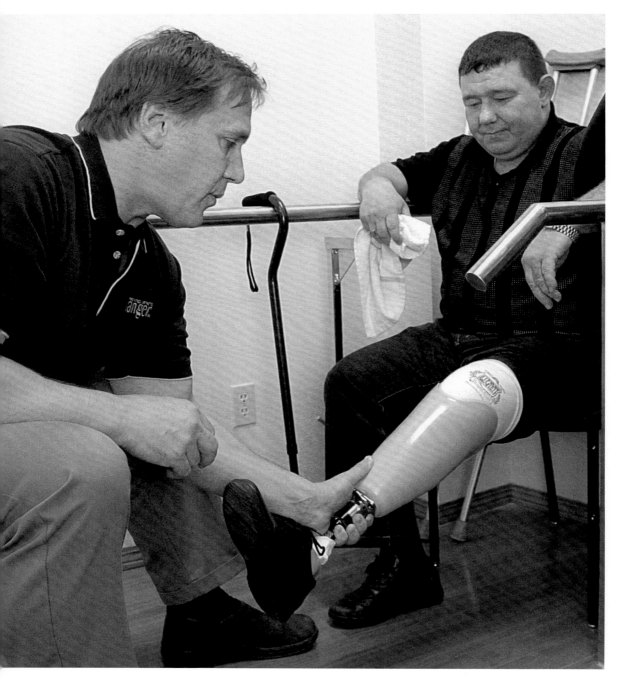

A prosthetist/orthotist checks a patient's new artificial leg. (Bob Zellar, *Billings Gazette*/AP Photo)

nology can be used to directly download specifications to an automated carver that manufactures the device.

Once the devices are made, orthotists and prosthetists fit them to their patients. They need to be creative in designing these devices and sympathetic in working with their patients. They must make any changes the patients need to comfortably wear the devices. After fitting, they will also help patients learn to use the artificial limbs or braces.

Prosthetists are also involved in the development and creation of myoelectric and externally powered prostheses. A patient with a myoelectric prosthesis can use the electrical impulses of his or her muscles to power a prosthetic limb. To accomplish this, an electrode is placed on the skin over a muscle. When the patient contracts that muscle, the electrode picks up and amplifies the electrical activity from the muscle. This

Words to Learn

AFO an abbreviation for "ankle-foot orthosis," which is a brace supporting this area

extremities the arms and legs

KAFO an abbreviation for "knee-ankle-foot orthosis," which is a brace supporting this area

myoelectrics the technology using electrical impulses from muscles to trigger a motorized part in a prosthesis, which then causes the prosthesis to move

orthosis a device applied to the outside of the body to immobilize or assist the motion of a specific part; an orthosis is usually called a brace

plaster cast model a form of a patient's body part, poured in plaster from the impressions taken by an orthotist or prosthetist

prosthesis a device used in place of a limb that is partially or completely missing

reliefs and build-ups pads of specified thickness that are placed in certain parts of the orthotic device

thermoforming using heat and sometimes pressure to shape a substance such as plastic

electrical signal then activates a battery-powered motor in the prosthetic that causes the device to move.

Orthotists and prosthetists usually work for hospitals and rehabilitation centers. Others work in nursing homes, specialty clinics, and home health settings. Some work in private practice. Orthotists and prosthetists also teach at colleges and universities.

To be a successful orthotist or prosthetist, you should have a strong desire to help people. You should have a creative personality and have the ability to visualize and invent. Other important traits include mechanical aptitude, computer skills, manual dexterity, an eye for detail, the ability to interact well with others, and strong communication skills.

Education and Training

High school courses in the sciences, psychology, mechanical drawing, computer-aided design, and shop will help you prepare for work in orthotics or prosthetics.

In the Beginning

Throughout history people have tried to replace lost limbs and support weak body parts. Braces, splints, and other corrective devices have been used since prehistoric times. Devices used during the Middle Ages included splints made out of leather for hips and legs, special shoes, and solid metal hands.

Some of the most dramatic advances made in the fields of prosthetics and orthotics have occurred during and after major wars. After World War II, for example, prosthetists discovered new lightweight plastics that could be used to make artificial arms and hands.

There is a great need for skilled workers in this field. More than 125,000 people lose a limb each year to illness or injury. Thousands of others have some sort of physical disability that requires orthotic assistance.

To become an orthotist or a prosthetist, you must go to college and earn a bachelor's degree. (By 2012, a minimum of a master's degree in orthotics and prosthetics will be required to work in these careers.) Typical college courses include Introduction to Orthotics and Prosthetics, Musculoskeletal System, Kinesiology, Plastics: Materials and Processes, Metals: Materials and Processes, Clinical Gait Analysis, Spinal and Upper Limb Orthotics, Lower Extremity Orthotics and Prosthetics, Spinal and Upper Extremity Orthotics and Prosthetics, Exercise Physiology for Rehabilitation Professionals, Psychological Aspects of Rehabilitation, and Administration of Orthotic and Prosthetic Facilities. You will also practice making and fitting devices in laboratories.

Many orthotists and prosthetists receive certification from the American Board for Certification in Orthotics, Prosthetics & Pedorthics (http://www.abcop.org) and the Board of Certification/Accreditation, International (http://www.bocusa.org).

DID YOU KNOW?

- The number of people who use a prosthesis is expected to reach 2.4 million by 2020.
- The number of people who use orthoses as a result of paralysis, deformity, or orthopedic impairments is expected to reach 7.3 million by 2020.
- More than 3,000 medical facilities in the United States provide orthotic and prosthetic services.

Sources: American Academy of Orthotists and Prosthetists, American Orthotic and Prosthetic Association, National Commission on Orthotic and Prosthetic Education

Earnings

Orthotists and prosthetists earned mean annual salaries of $66,600 in 2009, according to the U.S. Department of Labor. Those just starting out in the field earn less than $34,000, while workers with experience and advanced education can earn more than $104,000. Those who are certified and have worked in the field for at least 15 years can earn more than $95,667 a year, according to the American Orthotic and Prosthetic Association. Those who are not certified make less money.

FOR MORE INFO

For news related to the field, visit the academy's Web site.
American Academy of Orthotists and Prosthetists
1331 H Street, NW, Suite 501
Washington, DC 20005-4760
202-380-3663
http://www.oandp.org

For career and education information, contact
American Orthotic and Prosthetic Association
330 John Carlyle Street, Suite 200
Alexandria, VA 22314-5760
571-431-0876
info@aopanet.org
http://www.aopanet.org

For information on accredited schools, contact
National Commission on Orthotic and Prosthetic Education
330 John Carlyle Street, Suite 200
Alexandria, VA 22314-5760
703-836-7114
info@ncope.org
http://www.ncope.org

For more information about careers in orthotics and prosthetics, visit the following Web site:
Orthotics & Prosthetics: Make a Career of Making a Difference Everyday!
http://www.opcareers.org

Outlook

There will be excellent job opportunities for orthotists and prosthetists in the future. In fact, there is currently a shortage of trained professionals. According to *Issues Affecting the Future Demand for Orthotists and Prosthetists,* demand for orthotic services is expected to increase by 25 percent by 2020. Demand for prosthetic services is expected to increase 47 percent during this same time span. Demand is increasing because more people are being diagnosed with medical conditions or developing illnesses that create a need for orthotic and prosthetic devices. The growing number of soldiers who have lost limbs during combat is also increasing demand for orthotic and prosthetic professionals.

Physical Therapists

What Physical Therapists Do

Physical therapists help people who have been injured or ill to recover and relearn daily living skills, such as walking, eating, and bathing. They work with athletes who have been injured during a game or practice. They work with elderly people who have had accidents or strokes (an illness that occurs when a blood clot blocks an artery or a blood vessel). They also help children who have birth defects or disabilities. Physical therapists feel good when a person they are working with is able to do an activity he or she once did routinely.

Physical therapists first evaluate new patients to decide what treatment would help them. Physical therapists work as part of

EXPLORING

- Ask your teacher to arrange a visit to a physical therapy department at a hospital to see physical therapists at work.
- Read books on these subjects: massage, occupational therapy, arts therapy, anatomy, and physical therapy.
- Talk to a physical therapist

about his or her career. Ask the following questions: What made you want to enter this career? What are your typical hours? What do you like most and least about your job? How did you train for the field? What advice would you give to someone who is interested in the career?

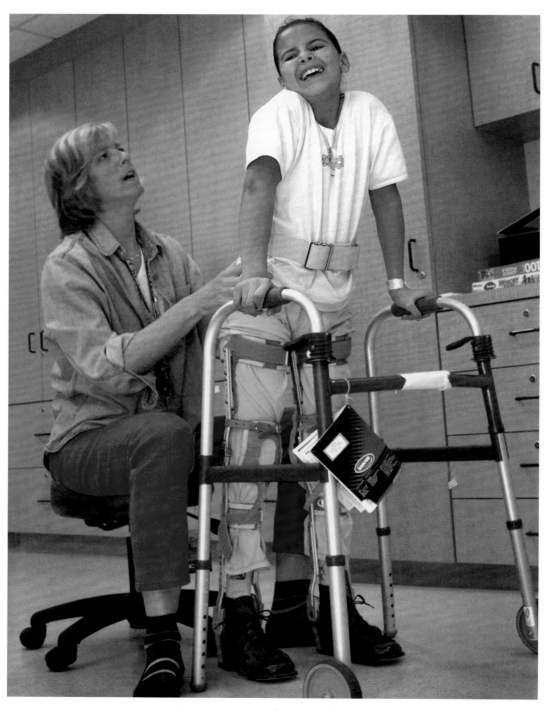

A physical therapist teaches a partially paralyzed young girl to walk again.
(Jacqueline R. Malonson, AP Photo)

a health care team that may include the patient's physician or surgeon, nurse, occupational therapist, and psychologist. After setting treatment goals for the patient, the physical therapist decides which methods to use.

If a patient has muscle damage in a leg, for example, the physical therapist may move the muscle through different motions and watch how the patient stands and walks to decide whether the patient needs braces or specific exercises. Other treatments often prescribed by therapists include hydrotherapy (the use of water in treatment), paraffin baths (a heat therapy used to treat arthritis and other joint conditions), infrared lamps, heating pads, ice, ultrasound, or electrical current.

Depending on the patient's injury or disability, therapy may last a few weeks, months, or even years. Physical therapists also teach patients and their families so that they can continue care at home.

Many physical therapists work in hospitals. Others work in private physical therapy offices, nursing homes, rehabilitation centers, schools, homes, sports medicine clinics, and industrial clinics. Some teach at colleges and universities. Others serve in the military.

Successful physical therapists like working with people and helping them feel better. They need creativity and patience to devise a treatment plan for each client and to help them achieve treatment goals. Physical therapists must also be willing to continue to learn throughout their careers. This field continues to change as new technology emerges and medical knowledge advances. They should also have a positive attitude and an outgoing and caring personality.

Education and Training

To prepare for a physical therapy career, you should take classes in health, biology, chemistry, and physics. Physical therapists work closely with clients every day. To improve your people and communication skills, take psychology, sociology, and Eng-

The Beginnings of Physical Therapy

During wartime, medical teams had to rehabilitate seriously injured soldiers. This contributed to the medical use and acceptance of physical therapy. The polio epidemic in the 1940s and 1950s, which left many victims paralyzed, also led to the demand for improved physical therapy.

DID YOU KNOW?

- In June 2009, females made up 74 percent of all licensed physical therapists, according to the American Physical Therapy Association.
- In June 2007, 32 percent of physical therapists were between the ages of 20 and 34, according to the American Physical Therapy Association.

lish and speech classes. Also, take computer science classes since physical therapists use computers and the Internet to keep records, create treatment plans, and stay up to date on developments in the field.

Physical therapists must earn at least a master's degree. Typical courses include anatomy, human growth and development, and therapeutic procedures. Students also gain hands-on experience (known as clinical experience) working with patients in hospitals, home care agencies, nursing homes, and other settings. Many earn postgraduate degrees. After graduation, you must pass an exam to become licensed. After a few years of work experience, you can earn a specialist certification. The American Board of Physical Therapy Specialties certifies physical therapists who show advanced knowledge in a specialty area. These specialties include cardiopulmonary, clinical electrophysiologic, geriatric, neurologic, orthopaedic, pediatric, and sports physical therapy.

Earnings

Physical therapists earned median annual salaries of $74,480 a year in 2009, according to the U.S. Department of Labor (DOL). The DOL reports the following mean salaries for physical therapists by employer: home health care services, $83,500; nursing care facilities, $78,990; offices of physicians, $77,120; offices of other health practitioners, $75,760; and general medical and surgical hospitals, $75,030. Those just starting out in the field earn less than $52,170. Experienced physical therapists can earn more than $105,900 annually.

Outlook

Employment in physical therapy is expected to be especially strong. As the number of middle-aged and elderly Americans grows, more people develop medical conditions that require physical therapy. As people live longer and more trauma victims and newborns with defects survive, the need for physical therapists rises. Additionally, people are becoming more interested in physical fitness. While this is a good thing, this trend means that more members of the public will need physical therapy to deal with the injuries they get while exercising.

FOR MORE INFO

The association offers the brochure *Your Career In Physical Therapy,* a directory of accredited schools, and general career information at its Web site.
American Physical Therapy Association
1111 North Fairfax Street
Alexandria, VA 22314-1488
800-999-2782
http://www.apta.org

Physicians

What Physicians Do

Physicians examine people to see if they are sick or well. If they are sick or injured, they decide on the treatment they need. Physicians must know all about how the body works and, when it does not work properly, they must know the possible ways to heal it.

Physicians hold either a doctor of medicine (M.D.) or osteopathic medicine (D.O.) degree. There is a good chance that your doctor is an M.D. In fact, about 80 percent of physicians are M.D.s. Like medical doctors, osteopathic physicians are fully trained and licensed to perform all aspects of medical care—including complex diagnosis, surgery, and the prescription of drugs. But osteopaths are different from traditional doctors. They practice traditional medicine with a special emphasis on your musculoskeletal system—your bones, muscles, and ligaments. Because osteopaths use the same medical and surgical procedures as other types of medical doctors, you can expect a visit to an osteopath to be much like a visit to any doctor.

Most physicians work in private practice. They see patients by appointment in their offices and in hospitals if they have serious illnesses. Many physicians are *general* or *family practitioners* who provide medical services to families and individuals of all ages and both sexes, usually on a regular basis. They perform routine check-ups, treat patients when they are sick or injured, and give advice about diet, exercise, and other health-related matters. Family practitioners can diagnose and treat most ail-

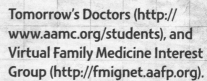

EXPLORING

- Visit the following Web sites to learn more about physicians: Tomorrow's Doctors (http://www.aamc.org/students/start.htm), AspiringDocs.org (http://www.aspiringdocs.org), Careers in Health Care (http://www.ama-assn.org/ama/pub/education-careers/careers-health-care.shtml), ExploreHealthCareers.org (http://explorehealthcareers.org), How Stuff Works: How Emergency Rooms Work (http://people.howstuffworks.com/emergency-room.htm), Human Anatomy Online (http://www.innerbody.com/htm/body.htm), Sloan Career Cornerstone Center: Medicine (http://www.careercornerstone.org/medicine/medicine.htm), The Student Doctor Network (http://www.studentdoctor.net), Tomorrow's Doctors (http://www.aamc.org/students), and Virtual Family Medicine Interest Group (http://fmignet.aafp.org).
- In high school, you might be able to volunteer at a local hospital, clinic, or nursing home. This is a good way to learn what it's like to work around other health care professionals and patients.
- Read as much as possible about the profession, including books on anatomy, medicines, diseases, health and fitness, and nutrition. See the Browse and Learn More section for a list of books about human anatomy and careers for physicians.
- Take a class in first aid and CPR.
- Ask you counselor or teacher to arrange an information interview with a physician.

ments. Some family practitioners set broken bones, deliver babies, or perform minor surgery.

When the patient's problem is severe or unusual, the family practitioner sends the patient to a physician who specializes in that disorder. For example, *cardiologists* take care of patients with heart disease. *Dermatologists* treat diseases and problems of the skin, hair, and nails. *Internists* treat diseases and injuries of the internal organs, including the lungs, stomach, and kidneys. *Pediatricians* care for children from birth to approximately the teenage years. *Gynecologists* and *obstetricians* are concerned with the health of a woman's reproductive system. They treat diseases and also provide care before, during, and after childbirth. *Geriatricians* treat the elderly and the disorders common to old age. *Surgeons* perform operations that repair injuries, help prevent disease, and improve the health of a patient. *Anesthesiologists* use medication to makes sure the patient feels no pain and remains uninjured during surgery. There are many other medical specialties. See the sidebar "Physician Specialty Associations on the Web" for more information.

Physicians work in hospitals, nursing homes, managed care offices, prisons, schools and universities, research laboratories, trauma centers, clinics, public health centers, and pharmaceu-

Profile: Hippocrates (460 B.C.–370 B.C.)

The first great physician was Hippocrates, a Greek who lived almost 2,500 years ago. He developed theories about medicine and the anatomy of the human body. But Hippocrates is remembered today for a set of medical ethics that still influences medical practice. The Hippocratic oath that he administered to his disciples is still given in a slightly different variation to new physicians today. His 87 essays on medicine, known as the "Hippocratic Collection," are believed to be the first record of early medical theory and practice. Hippocratic physicians believed that health was maintained by a proper balance of four "humors" in the body: blood, phlegm, black bile, and yellow bile.

tical and chemical companies. Some are self-employed in their own or group practices. There are also positions available in government agencies such as the Centers for Disease Control, the Food and Drug Administration, and the National Institutes of Health.

Education and Training

You must study and train for many years before you can become a physician. If you want to become a doctor, you should take high school college-preparatory courses, including English, a foreign language, social studies, mathematics, biology, anatomy, chemistry, physics, and computer science. Also while in high school, volunteering in a hospital or medical office is good experience.

Tips for Success

To be a successful physician, you should

- have a desire to help others
- have compassion for those who are sick or injured
- be very good at science
- have excellent communication skills
- be a good listener
- be able to think quickly during emergencies
- be willing to continue to learn throughout your career

After high school, you must attend college. A premed program is ideal, but you can major in any subject. It is important, though, to take science courses.

After college, you must go to medical school. In the first two years of medical school, you will learn about human anatomy, physiology, human cells, and prescription drugs. Osteopathic medical students take these classes, but also take courses that focus on the ways in which the musculoskeletal and nervous systems influence the functioning of the entire body. During the last two years, you will spend time in a hospital and become part of a medical team. Beginning with basic tasks, you learn medical skills by practicing them under the close supervision of licensed physicians. You may take personal histories from patients, make diagnoses, and perform laboratory tests. You also learn about medical specialties, such as pediatrics, psychiatry, obstetrics and gynecology, geriatrics, surgery, and family practice. After you complete the four years of study, you will participate in internships in areas such as internal medicine, obstetrics/gynecology, and surgery.

Once you receive your doctor of medicine or doctor of osteopathic medicine degree, you must pass a test to be licensed to practice. Most physicians then complete from one to three more years of training, usually as hospital residents or interns. If you wish to become a specialist, you will spend another one to seven years in training.

Earnings

Physicians have among the highest earnings of any occupation. According to the Medical Group Management Association, the median income for all physicians is about $186,000 a year. The U.S. Department of Labor reports the following mean annual earnings for physicians by specialty in 2009: general surgeons, $219,770; anesthesiologists, $211,750; obstetricians/gynecologists, $204,470; and pediatricians, $161,410. Salaries for family medicine practitioners ranged from $82,630 to more than $166,400.

Outlook

Employment for physicians is expected to be very good during the next decade. Population growth, especially among the elderly, will increase the demand for physicians. People are also living longer, which is creating more need for physicians. Employment will be especially strong for family practitioners, internists, geriatric and preventive care specialists, and general pediatricians.

FOR MORE INFO

Visit the academy's Web site to access career information and other resources.
American Academy of Family Physicians
PO Box 11210
Shawnee Mission, KS 66207-1210
800-274-2237
contactcenter@aafp.org
http://www.aafp.org

To read the *Osteopathic Medical College Information Book*, visit the association's Web site.
American Association of Colleges of Osteopathic Medicine
5550 Friendship Boulevard, Suite 310
Chevy Chase, MD 20815-7231
301-968-4100
http://www.aacom.org

For general information about health care careers, contact
American Medical Association
515 North State Street
Chicago, IL 60654-4854
800-621-8335
http://www.ama-assn.org

For information about osteopathic medicine, visit the association's Web site.
American Osteopathic Association
142 East Ontario Street
Chicago, IL 60611-2874
800-621-1773
http://www.osteopathic.org

For a list of accredited U.S. and Canadian medical schools and other education information, contact
Association of American Medical Colleges
2450 N Street, NW
Washington, DC 20037-1126
202-828-0400
http://www.aamc.org

There is strong competition for jobs—especially in big cities. Physicians are in short supply in rural and low-income areas. Physicians who are willing to practice in these places will have excellent opportunities.

Many people want to become physicians, so it is very hard to enter this field. Students with high grades throughout their school years will have the best chances of being accepted into medical school.

Psychiatrists

What Psychiatrists Do

Psychiatrists are physicians who treat and prevent mental illness. They work with people of all ages who might have feelings of anger or fear, or people who are so confused that they have completely lost touch with reality. Psychiatrists use a variety of methods to treat patients. They might discuss problems, prescribe medicine, or combine discussions, medication, and other types of therapy.

Mental illness has several possible causes. A mental problem might be caused by a physical disorder. It might be caused by a person's inability to handle stress and conflict. Some disorders are only temporary while others last a long time. People with mental problems cannot do certain things because of the way they think, feel, or act. Whenever possible, psychiatrists help these people overcome their problems and lead happier lives.

To determine the cause of a mental illness, psychiatrists interview patients. Then they give them complete physical examinations. To understand patients, a psychiatrist must learn about important events in their lives and any strong feelings or opin-

EXPLORING

- Read all you can about psychiatry. Ask your school or community librarian to suggest some books and magazines.
- Visit the Web sites of psychology associations.
- Talk with your school counselors and ask them for information about psychiatry careers.
- Ask your psychology teacher or a counselor to arrange an information interview with a psychiatrist.

ions they have toward others. Many times a psychiatrist can improve a patient's condition by helping him or her understand why a problem has occurred. Together, the psychiatrist and patient then find other ways for the patient to think and behave. This process is called psychotherapy. In cases where discussing a problem is not enough, or when serious mental problems are caused by a brain disorder, a psychiatrist may prescribe medication.

About half of practicing psychiatrists work in private practice. Many others combine private practice with work in a health care institution. These institutions include private hospitals, state mental hospitals, medical schools, community health centers, and government health agencies. Psychiatrists may also work at correctional facilities, for health maintenance organizations, or in nursing homes.

The psychiatrist's work can be emotionally demanding. Psychiatrists spend much of their time with people who are depressed and angry. Some patients may even be suicidal (want to kill themselves). It is important that psychiatrists have an even-keeled personality in order to effectively work with challenging patients. Psychiatrists must be good listeners and be able to work well with others. They must also be willing to continue to learn throughout their careers since new therapies and medications are constantly being developed.

Education and Training

In high school, take a college preparatory curriculum that includes classes in biology, chemistry, physics, algebra, geometry, and calculus. You should also start learning about human behavior by taking psychology, sociology, and history classes.

You need many years of schooling and experience to become a psychiatrist. After you graduate from a four-year college, you must enter a four-year program at a medical school. These programs provide extensive training in anatomy, biology, medical practices,

Words to Learn

neurosis an emotional disorder that arises due to unresolved conflicts; anxiety is often the main characteristic

phobia a persistent, unrealistic fear of an object or situation

psychoanalysis a method of treating mental disorders by bringing unconscious fears and conflicts into the conscious mind

psychosis a major mental disorder, in which the personality is seriously disorganized and the person loses contact with reality

psychosomatic a physical illness caused or made worse by a mental condition

psychotherapy the treatment of mental disorders by psychological, rather than physical, means

and other subjects. After graduating from medical school, you must pass exams to become a medical doctor. You then complete at least four additional years of training in the treatment of the mentally ill. You study medical practices, but mostly you train on-the-job at a psychiatric hospital. You are closely supervised by experienced psychiatrists during this time.

Before you can begin to practice as a psychiatrist, you must become licensed as a physician.

DID YOU KNOW?

The American Academy of Child and Adolescent Psychiatry reports that, at any one time, between seven and 12 million youths in the United States suffer from mental, behavioral, or developmental disorders.

Earnings

Psychiatrists' earnings depend on the kind of practice they have and its location, their experience, and the number of patients they treat. Psychiatrists earned median annual salaries of $160,230 in 2009, according to the U.S. Department of Labor. Salaries for psychiatrists ranged from $65,590 to more than $199,910.

FOR MORE INFO

For information about child and adolescent psychiatry, contact
American Academy of Child and Adolescent Psychiatry
3615 Wisconsin Avenue, NW
Washington, DC 20016-3007
202-966-730
http://www.aacap.org

For information about geriatric psychiatry, contact
American Association for Geriatric Psychiatry
7910 Woodmont Avenue, Suite 1050
Bethesda, MD 20814-3004
301-654-7850
main@aagponline.org
http://www.aagpgpa.org

For more information on becoming a doctor as well as current health care news, visit the AMA Web site.
American Medical Association (AMA)
515 North State Street

Chicago, IL 60654-4854
800-621-8335
http://www.ama-assn.org

For detailed information about careers in psychiatry, contact
American Psychiatric Association
1000 Wilson Boulevard, Suite 1825
Arlington, VA 22209-3901
888-357-7924
apa@psych.org
http://www.psych.org

For information about mental health issues, contact
National Institute of Mental Health
Science Writing, Press, and Dissemination Branch
6001 Executive Boulevard, Room 8184, MSC 9663
Bethesda, MD 20892-9663
866-615-6464
nimhinfo@nih.gov
http://www.nimh.nih.gov

Outlook

During the next decade there will be a strong demand for skilled psychiatrists. A growing population and increasing life spans mean more people will need psychiatric care. Rising incomes allow more people to afford treatment. A shortage of psychiatrists, especially for children and in rural areas, will keep job opportunities bright for the next decade.

Glossary

accredited approved as meeting established standards for providing good training and education; this approval is usually given by an independent organization of professionals

annual salary the money an individual earns for an entire year of work

apprentice a person who is learning a trade by working under the supervision of a skilled worker; apprentices often receive classroom instruction in addition to their supervised practical experience

associate's degree an academic rank or title granted by a community or junior college or similar institution to graduates of a two-year program of education beyond high school

bachelor's degree an academic rank or title given to a person who has completed a four-year program of study at a college or university; also called an **undergraduate degree** or **baccalaureate.**

career an occupation for which a worker receives training and has an opportunity for advancement

certified approved as meeting established requirements for skill, knowledge, and experience in a particular field; people are certified by an organization of professionals in their field

college a higher education institution that is above the high school level

community college a public or private two-year college attended by students who do not usually live at the college; graduates of a community college receive an associate's degree and may transfer to a four-year college or university to complete a bachelor's degree

diploma a certificate or document given by a school to show that a person has completed a course or has graduated from the school

distance education a type of educational program that allows students to take classes and complete their education by mail or the Internet

doctorate   the highest academic rank or title granted by a graduate school to a person who has completed a two- to three-year program after having received a master's degree.

fellowship   a financial award given for research projects or dissertation assistance; fellowships are commonly offered at the graduate, postgraduate, or doctoral levels

freelancer   a worker who is not a regular employee of a company; they work for themselves and do not receive a regular paycheck

fringe benefit   a payment or benefit to an employee in addition to regular wages or salary; examples of fringe benefits include a pension, a paid vacation, and health or life insurance

graduate school   a school that people may attend after they have received their bachelor's degree; people who complete an educational program at a graduate school earn a master's degree or a doctorate

intern   an advanced student (usually one with at least some college training) in a professional field who is employed in a job that is intended to provide supervised practical experience for the student

internship   1. The position or job of an intern; 2. The period of time when a person is an intern

junior college   a two-year college that offers courses like those in the first half of a four-year college program; graduates of a junior college usually receive an associate's degree and may transfer to a four-year college or university to complete a bachelor's degree

liberal arts   the subjects covered by college courses that develop broad general knowledge rather than specific occupational skills; the liberal arts are often considered to include philosophy, literature and the arts, history, language, and some courses in the social sciences and natural sciences

major (in college)   the academic field in which a student specializes and receives a degree

master's degree   an academic rank or title granted by a graduate school to a person who has completed a one- or two-year program after having received a bachelor's degree

medical degree   a degree awarded to an individual who has completed four years of training at a medical school

medical school   a school that students attend in order to become a physician; people who complete an educational program at a medical school earn either a doctor of medicine (M.D.) or osteopathic medicine (D.O.) degree

pension   an amount of money paid regularly by an employer to a former employee after he or she retires from working

scholarship   a gift of money to a student to help the student pay for further education

social studies   courses of study (such as civics, geography, and history) that deal with how human societies work

starting salary   salary paid to a newly hired employee; the starting salary is usually a smaller amount than is paid to a more experienced worker

technical college   a private or public college offering two- or four-year programs in technical subjects; technical colleges offer courses in both general and technical subjects and award associate's degrees and bachelor's degrees

undergraduate   student at a college or university who has not yet received a degree

undergraduate degree   see **bachelor's degree**

union   an organization whose members are workers in a particular industry or company; the union works to gain better wages, benefits, and working conditions for its members; also called a **labor union** or **trade union**

vocational school   a public or private school that offers training in one or more skills or trades

wage   money that is paid in return for work done, especially money paid on the basis of the number of hours or days worked

Browse and Learn More

Books

Asher, Dana. *Epidemiologists: Life Tracking Deadly Diseases.* New York: Rosen Publishing Group, 2002.

Bailey, Diane. *Brain Surgeons.* New York: Rosen Publishing Group, 2009.

Ballard, Carol. *Exploring the Human Body: The Brain and Nervous System.* Farmington Hills, Mich.: KidHaven Press, 2005.

Ballard, Carol. *Exploring the Human Body: The Heart and Circulation.* Farmington Hills, Mich.: KidHaven Press, 2005.

Ballard, Carol. *Exploring the Human Body: The Lungs and Respiration.* Farmington Hills, Mich.: KidHaven Press, 2005.

Ballard, Carol. *Exploring the Human Body: The Skeleton and Muscles.* Farmington Hills, Mich.: KidHaven Press, 2005.

Ballard, Carol. *Exploring the Human Body: The Stomach and Digestion.* Farmington Hills, Mich.: KidHaven Press, 2005.

Bowles, Roger. *Biomedical Equipment Technicians.* Waco, Tex.: TSTC Publishing, 2008.

Buchbinder, Sharon B., and Nancy H. Shanks. *Introduction to Health Care Management.* Sudbury, Mass.: Jones & Bartlett Publishers, 2007.

Christe, Barbara. *Introduction to Biomedical Instrumentation: The Technology of Patient Care.* New York: Cambridge University Press, 2009.

Cobb, Allan B. *First Responders.* New York: Rosen Publishing Group, 2007.

Floyd, Patricia A., and Beverly Allen. *Careers in Health, Physical Education, and Sports.* 2d ed. Florence, K.Y.: Brooks Cole, 2008.

Frederickson, Keville. *Opportunities in Nursing Careers.* 2d ed. New York: McGraw-Hill Companies, 2003.

Fuzy, Jetta, and William Leahy. *The Home Health Aide Handbook.* 2d ed. Albuquerque, N.Mex.: Hartman Publishing Inc., 2005.

Gingerich, Barbara Stover, and Deborah Anne Ondeck. *Pocket Guide for the Home Care Aide.* 2d ed. Sudbury, Mass.: Jones & Bartlett Publishers, 2008.

Green, Michelle A., and Mary Jo Bowie. *Essentials of Health Information Management: Principles and Practices.* Florence, Ky.: Delmar Cengage Learning, 2007.

Haddock, Cynthia Carter, Robert C. Chapman, and Robert A. McLean. *Careers in Healthcare Management: How to Find Your Path and Follow It.* Chicago: Health Administration Press, 2002.

Katz, Janet. *A Career in Nursing: Is It Right For Me?* St. Louis: Mosby, 2007.

Kendall, Bonnie. *Opportunities in Dental Care Careers.* New York: McGraw-Hill, 2006.

Kummer, Patricia K. *Sports Medicine Doctor.* Ann Arbor, Mich.: Cherry Lake Publishing, 2008.

Littlejohn, Randy. *Careers in Fitness and Personal Training.* New York: Rosen Publishing Group, 2005.

Miller, Michaela. *Exploring the Human Body: Reproduction and Growth.* Farmington Hills, Mich.: KidHaven Press, 2005.

Novotny, Jeanne M., Doris T. Lippman, Nicole K. Sanders, and Joyce J. Fitzpatrick. *101 Careers in Nursing.* New York: Springer Publishing Company, 2006.

Pagliarulo, Michael A. *Introduction to Physical Therapy.* 3d ed. St. Louis: C.V. Mosby, 2006.

Peterson's. *Peterson's Summer Opportunities for Kids & Teenagers.* 26th ed. Lawrenceville, N.J.: Peterson's, 2008.

Sorrentino, Sheila A., Leighann Remmert, and Bernie Gorek. *Mosby's Essentials for Nursing Assistants.* 4th ed. St. Louis: Mosby, 2009.

Thompson, Tamara. *Careers for the Twenty-First Century: Emergency Response.* Farmington Hills, Mich.: Lucent Books, 2004.

Tilden, Thomasine E. Lewis. *24-7 Medical Files: Help! What's Eating My Flesh?* New York: Children's Press, 2007.

Vallano, Annette. *Your Career in Nursing: Manage Your Future in the Changing World of Healthcare.* 5th ed. New York: Kaplan Publishing, 2008.

Wynbrandt, James. *The Excruciating History of Dentistry: Toothsome Tales & Oral Oddities from Babylon to Braces.* New York: St. Martin's Griffin, 2000.

Young, Audrey. *What Patients Taught Me: A Medical Student's Journey.* Seattle: Sasquatch Books, 2007.

Periodicals

Advance for Nurses
http://nursing.advanceweb.com

The American Nurse
http://www.nursingworld.org/tan

American Family Physician
http://www.aafp.org/online/en/home/publications/journals/afp.html

American Orthotic and Prosthetic Association Almanac
http://www.aopanet.org/op_almanac/index.php

The Bell
http://www.nmha.org/go/pressroom/bell

Biomedical Instrumentation & Technology
http://www.aami.org/publications/BIT/index.html

Caring
http://digitalcaringmagazine.nahc.org

Journal of the American Medical Association
http://jama.ama-assn.org

Journal of the American Physical Therapy Association
http://ptjournal.apta.org

The Pre-Engineering Times
http://www.jets.org/newsletter/index.cfm

Web Sites

American Dental Association: ADA for Kids
http://www.ada.org/353.aspx

American Dental Association: Dentistry Career Options
http://www.ada.org/3324.aspx

American Dental Hygienists' Association: Kids Stuff
http://www.adha.org/kidstuff

American Dietetic Association: Center for Career Opportunities
http://www.eatright.org/FNCE/content.aspx?id=416

American Library Association: Great Web Sites for Kids
http://www.ala.org/greatsites

AspiringDocs.org
http://www.aspiringdocs.org

BAM! Body & Mind
http://www.bam.gov

The Biomedical Engineering Network
http://www.bmenet.org

Careers in Health Care
http://www.ama-assn.org/ama/pub/education-careers/careers-health-care.shtml

Careers in Pathology and Medical Laboratory Science
http://www.ascp.org/pdf/CareerBooklet.aspx

Discover Nursing
http://www.discovernursing.com

Discovery Health: How Emergency Rooms Work
http://health.howstuffworks.com/medicine/healthcare-providers/emergency-room.htm

Dr. Samuel D. Harris National Museum of Dentistry
http://www.dentalmuseum.org

ExploreHealthCareers.org
http://explorehealthcareers.org

4,000 Years of Women in Science
http://www.astr.ua.edu/4000WS

Human Anatomy Online
http://www.innerbody.com/htm/body.html

Human Genome Project Information
http://www.ornl.gov/sci/techresources/Human_Genome/home.
html

Infection Detection Protection
http://www.amnh.org/nationalcenter/infection

Kidnetic.com
http://www.kidnetic.com

Kids.gov
http://www.kids.gov

KidsCamps.com
http://www.kidscamps.com

KidsHealth
http://kidshealth.org

Make a Difference: Discover a Career in Healthcare Management!
http://www.healthmanagementcareers.org

Mouth Power Online
http://www.mouthpower.org

MyPyramid.gov
http://www.mypyramid.gov

The *New York Times* on the Web Learning Network
http://learning.blogs.nytimes.com

Nutrition.gov
http://www.nutrition.gov

Sloan Career Cornerstone Center: Medicine
http://www.careercornerstone.org/medicine/medicine.htm

The Student Doctor Network
http://www.studentdoctor.net

Tomorrow's Doctors
http://www.aamc.org/students

U.S. Department of Health and Human Services for Kids
http://www.hhs.gov/kids

U.S. Food and Drug Administration For Kids
http://www.fda.gov/ForConsumers/ByAudience/ForKids

Virtual Family Medicine Interest Group
http://fmignet.aafp.org/online/fmig/index.html

Visit the Dentist with Marty
http://www.ada.org/379.aspx

Your Career in Chiropractic
http://www.acatoday.org/pdf/CareerKit.pdf

Your Career in Physical Therapy
http://www.apta.org/AM/Template.cfm?Section=A_Career_in_Physical_Therapy&Template=/TaggedPage/TaggedPageDisplay.cfm&TPLID=242&ContentID=29277

Index